Holographic Worlds

Kai Ba's Immersive Environments

Priya Costa

ISBN: 9781779666109
Imprint: Press for Play Books
Copyright © 2024 Priya Costa.
All Rights Reserved.

Contents

The Birth of an Innovator   1
Early Life and Influences   1

Bibliography   11
Education and Formative Experiences   14
Enter the World of Immersion   27

The Revolution Begins   41
Founding the Immersive Environments Lab   41

Bibliography   47
Development of the Holographic Worlds Platform   55
Applications in Various Fields   68

Bibliography   71

Facing Challenges and Changing the World   81
Holographic Worlds Beyond Earth   81
Ethical Considerations and Social Impact   94
Future Innovations and Societal Paradigm Shifts   107

Kai Ba's Legacy and Reflections   119
Impact on Future Generations   119

Bibliography   123
Personal Growth and Lessons Learned   132

Bibliography   139

Epilogue: The Future of Holographic Worlds   147

The Evolution of Immersive Environments 147

Index 161

Contents

The Birth of an Innovator　1
Early Life and Influences　1

Bibliography　11
Education and Formative Experiences　14
Enter the World of Immersion　27

The Revolution Begins　41
Founding the Immersive Environments Lab　41

Bibliography　47
Development of the Holographic Worlds Platform　55
Applications in Various Fields　68

Bibliography　71

Facing Challenges and Changing the World　81
Holographic Worlds Beyond Earth　81
Ethical Considerations and Social Impact　94
Future Innovations and Societal Paradigm Shifts　107

Kai Ba's Legacy and Reflections　119
Impact on Future Generations　119

Bibliography　123
Personal Growth and Lessons Learned　132

Bibliography　139

Epilogue: The Future of Holographic Worlds　147

The Evolution of Immersive Environments 147

Index 161

The Birth of an Innovator

Early Life and Influences

A Childhood of Curiosity

Kai Ba's childhood was characterized by an insatiable curiosity that would lay the groundwork for his future innovations in immersive environments. Growing up in a small town, he was surrounded by the natural world, which sparked his interest in science and technology from an early age. This section explores the key influences and experiences during his formative years that shaped his inquisitive mind.

The Early Spark of Curiosity

From the moment he could walk, Kai was known for his tendency to dismantle household appliances, much to the dismay of his parents. This innate desire to understand how things worked was not just a phase; it was a manifestation of his deep-rooted curiosity. According to Piaget's theory of cognitive development, children learn through active exploration of their environment [?]. Kai embodied this concept, often spending hours in the garage with his father, who was a mechanic, learning the intricacies of engines and machinery.

Influence of Family

Kai's family played a crucial role in nurturing his curiosity. His mother, an elementary school teacher, encouraged him to ask questions and seek answers. She often brought home science kits and books that introduced him to the wonders of physics and biology. One particular instance stands out: when she gifted him a telescope for his tenth birthday. This gift not only ignited his passion for astronomy but also reinforced the idea that the universe was full of mysteries waiting to be uncovered.

Mentorship and Guidance

In addition to his parents, Kai was fortunate to have mentors who recognized his potential. One such figure was Mr. Thompson, his high school science teacher, who introduced him to the world of robotics. Under Mr. Thompson's guidance, Kai joined the school's robotics club, where he learned to design and program robots. This experience was pivotal; it not only honed his technical skills but also taught him the importance of teamwork and collaboration.

Inspirations from Science Fiction

Kai's love for science fiction literature further fueled his curiosity. Books like Isaac Asimov's *Foundation* series and Arthur C. Clarke's *Rendezvous with Rama* opened his mind to the possibilities of technology and the future. These narratives inspired him to think beyond the constraints of his reality and envision a world where technology could create immersive experiences. The concept of virtual worlds, as depicted in these stories, became a driving force in his aspirations.

The Impact of Virtual Reality

As a teenager, Kai was introduced to early virtual reality (VR) systems through a local tech fair. The experience of donning a VR headset and being transported to another world was transformative. This encounter solidified his desire to explore the intersection of technology and human experience. The potential of VR to create immersive environments captivated him, leading him to dream of a future where such technologies could revolutionize education, entertainment, and beyond.

Exploring Different Cultures

Kai's curiosity was not limited to technology; he also had a profound interest in different cultures. His parents often took him on trips to various countries, exposing him to diverse ways of life and perspectives. These experiences instilled in him a sense of empathy and a desire to create technologies that could bridge cultural divides. He believed that understanding and appreciating different cultures was essential in designing immersive environments that resonated with a global audience.

Conclusion

In conclusion, Kai Ba's childhood was marked by a relentless curiosity that was nurtured by his family, mentors, and experiences. His early fascination with how things worked, combined with influences from science fiction and exposure to different cultures, set the stage for his future innovations in holographic worlds. This foundation of curiosity would prove to be a driving force in his journey as an innovator, shaping his vision of a future where technology could enhance human experiences in profound ways.

Family and Mentorship

Kai Ba's journey into the realm of innovation was significantly shaped by the strong familial bonds and mentorship he received throughout his formative years. The interplay between family influence and mentorship is crucial in nurturing a young innovator's potential. This section explores the impact of Kai's family background and the mentors who guided him on his path to becoming a pioneer in immersive environments.

Family Influence

Kai was born into a family that valued creativity and intellectual curiosity. His parents, both educators, instilled in him a love for learning from an early age. They encouraged him to explore various subjects, fostering an environment where questions were welcomed, and knowledge was pursued passionately. This nurturing atmosphere was pivotal in shaping Kai's inquisitive nature, allowing him to develop a sense of wonder that would fuel his future innovations.

The concept of family influence can be examined through the lens of social learning theory, which posits that individuals learn behaviors and norms through observation and imitation of others, particularly those they are close to. Bandura's (1977) work highlights the importance of role models in shaping an individual's attitudes and behaviors. In Kai's case, his parents served as exemplary role models, demonstrating the value of education and the pursuit of knowledge. This foundational support allowed Kai to envision a future where he could contribute to technological advancements.

Mentorship: A Guiding Light

In addition to his family, Kai was fortunate to encounter several mentors throughout his educational journey. Mentorship plays a critical role in personal and professional development, providing guidance, support, and encouragement. According to Kram (1985), mentorship can be categorized into two types: career functions and psychosocial functions. Career functions include sponsorship, exposure, and coaching, while psychosocial functions encompass role modeling, acceptance, and counseling.

One of Kai's most influential mentors was Dr. Elena Torres, a renowned researcher in virtual reality. Dr. Torres recognized Kai's potential early on and took him under her wing during his undergraduate studies. She provided him with opportunities to engage in groundbreaking research projects, fostering his technical skills and critical thinking abilities. Through her mentorship, Kai learned the importance of perseverance in the face of challenges and the value of collaboration in innovation.

The relationship between Kai and Dr. Torres exemplifies the significance of mentorship in fostering innovation. Research shows that individuals with mentors are more likely to pursue ambitious career paths and achieve higher levels of success (Eby et al., 2008). Dr. Torres not only guided Kai in his academic pursuits but also encouraged him to think outside the box, pushing the boundaries of traditional approaches to technology.

Challenges and Growth

Despite the strong support from his family and mentors, Kai faced numerous challenges on his journey. The pressure to excel in a competitive academic environment often led to self-doubt and anxiety. This phenomenon aligns with the concept of imposter syndrome, where individuals feel inadequate despite their accomplishments (Clance & Imes, 1978). Kai's mentors played a crucial role in helping him navigate these feelings, providing reassurance and reinforcing his capabilities.

Moreover, the evolving nature of technology presented Kai with obstacles that required adaptability and resilience. The fast-paced advancements in virtual and augmented reality demanded continuous learning and innovation. His family's encouragement to embrace failure as a learning opportunity became a vital mantra in overcoming setbacks. This mindset is echoed in Dweck's (2006) research on growth mindset, which emphasizes the belief that abilities can be developed through dedication and hard work.

Conclusion

The influence of family and mentorship in Kai Ba's life cannot be overstated. His parents' unwavering support and the guidance of mentors like Dr. Elena Torres provided him with the tools and confidence necessary to pursue his passion for technology. As Kai embarked on his journey to revolutionize immersive environments, the lessons learned from his family and mentors remained integral to his growth as an innovator. The synthesis of familial encouragement and mentorship exemplifies the collaborative nature of personal development, highlighting the importance of community in fostering the next generation of innovators.

In summary, Kai's experiences underscore the profound impact that family and mentorship can have on an individual's journey toward innovation. As he continued to explore the potential of holographic worlds, the foundational values instilled by his family and the guidance of his mentors shaped his vision and aspirations, propelling him toward a future of limitless possibilities.

Inspirations from Science Fiction

Science fiction has long served as a fertile ground for imagination and innovation, providing a canvas upon which the dreams of futurists can be painted. For Kai Ba, the influence of science fiction was not merely a source of entertainment but a profound catalyst that shaped his vision of immersive environments. This section delves into the pivotal works of science fiction that inspired Kai, the theoretical frameworks that emerged from these narratives, and the problems they posed, all of which contributed to his groundbreaking innovations in holographic technology.

Theoretical Frameworks and Concepts

Science fiction often explores theoretical constructs that challenge our understanding of reality. Concepts such as virtual reality, artificial intelligence, and interstellar travel are not just fanciful tales; they often embody theoretical frameworks that scientists and technologists grapple with in the real world. For instance, the idea of a digital universe, as explored in works like *Neuromancer* by William Gibson, introduces the concept of cyberspace—a term that has since become integral to discussions about the internet and virtual environments.

Theoretical physicist David Deutsch, in his book *The Beginning of Infinity*, argues that the universe is fundamentally computable. This idea resonates with the premise of many science fiction narratives that suggest our reality could be a simulation. Such theories push innovators like Kai Ba to consider the implications of creating immersive environments that mimic or even surpass our own reality.

Key Inspirations from Science Fiction

Several seminal works of science fiction have left a lasting impact on Kai Ba's approach to technology:

- **Arthur C. Clarke's *2001: A Space Odyssey***: The depiction of HAL 9000, an artificial intelligence that interacts with humans, raised questions about machine consciousness and ethics. Kai Ba drew inspiration from HAL's capabilities to envision how AI could enhance immersive environments, leading to the development of more intuitive user interfaces in holographic worlds.

- **Philip K. Dick's *Do Androids Dream of Electric Sheep?***: This narrative explores the nature of humanity and reality, prompting Kai to consider the ethical implications of virtual environments. The line between human experience and artificial constructs became a focal point in his work, leading to the incorporation of ethical considerations in the design of immersive experiences.

- **William Gibson's *Neuromancer***: The concept of cyberspace as a digital landscape inspired Kai to push the boundaries of virtual reality. The idea of navigating through a digital realm became a foundational element in the development of his holographic platforms, where users could interact with 3D environments in unprecedented ways.

- **Isaac Asimov's *I, Robot***: Asimov's exploration of robotics and the laws governing them influenced Kai's understanding of the responsibilities that come with technological advancement. The ethical frameworks proposed in Asimov's narratives guided Kai in creating holographic environments that prioritize user safety and agency.

Problems Posed by Science Fiction

While science fiction serves as an inspiration, it also presents a myriad of problems and dilemmas that innovators like Kai Ba must confront. These problems often reflect societal concerns and ethical quandaries that arise from technological advancements:

- **The Ethics of AI and Automation**: As seen in many science fiction narratives, the rise of AI poses significant ethical challenges. Kai Ba grappled with questions surrounding the autonomy of AI within immersive environments. How can we ensure that AI enhances human experience without infringing on personal freedoms?

- **The Nature of Reality**: The blurring lines between virtual and real worlds present a philosophical dilemma. As Kai developed holographic technologies, he considered the implications of users becoming overly immersed in virtual experiences at the expense of their real-world interactions. This concern is echoed in narratives like *Ready Player One* by Ernest Cline, where characters escape into a virtual utopia.

- **Social Inequality and Access:** Many science fiction stories highlight the disparities in access to technology. Kai Ba was acutely aware of the potential for holographic technologies to exacerbate existing inequalities. He sought to create inclusive platforms that would democratize access to immersive environments, ensuring that they are available to diverse populations.

Conclusion

In conclusion, the inspirations drawn from science fiction have been instrumental in shaping Kai Ba's vision of holographic worlds. The theoretical frameworks, key narratives, and ethical dilemmas presented in these works not only fueled his creativity but also grounded his innovations in a broader societal context. As Kai continues to push the boundaries of immersive environments, the lessons learned from science fiction serve as both a guiding light and a cautionary tale, reminding him of the profound responsibilities that accompany technological advancement.

Through this exploration, we see that science fiction is not merely a genre of storytelling; it is a powerful tool for innovation, urging us to dream boldly while remaining vigilant about the implications of our creations.

The Impact of Virtual Reality

Virtual Reality (VR) has emerged as a transformative technology that reshapes how individuals interact with digital environments. Its impact spans various domains, from entertainment to education, healthcare, and beyond. This section explores the multifaceted effects of VR on society, focusing on its theoretical underpinnings, practical applications, and the challenges it presents.

Theoretical Foundations of Virtual Reality

The concept of Virtual Reality is rooted in the idea of creating immersive experiences that simulate real or imagined environments. According to [Slater & Wilbur, 2009], immersion is defined as "the subjective experience of being in one place or another," which can be achieved through various sensory stimuli. The effectiveness of VR relies on several theories, including:

- **Presence Theory:** This theory posits that users feel a sense of presence in a virtual environment when they are fully engaged and immersed. [?] identified three key components that contribute to the sense of presence: sensory fidelity, interactivity, and the user's emotional response.

- **Flow Theory:** Proposed by [Csikszentmihalyi, 1990], this theory describes a state of complete absorption in an activity, leading to heightened enjoyment and creativity. VR can facilitate flow experiences by providing challenges that match the user's skill level.

- **Social Presence Theory:** This theory emphasizes the importance of social interactions in virtual environments. [Biocca et al., 2001] argues that the perception of others in VR can enhance the overall experience, making it more engaging and meaningful.

Applications of Virtual Reality

The applications of VR are vast and varied, significantly impacting numerous fields:

1. Entertainment and Gaming VR has revolutionized the gaming industry, allowing players to immerse themselves in rich, interactive worlds. Titles such as *Beat Saber* and *Half-Life: Alyx* showcase the potential of VR to provide unique gaming experiences that traditional platforms cannot replicate. According to [Dixon, 2019], VR gaming enhances user engagement and emotional responses, creating a more profound connection to the game narrative.

2. Education and Training In education, VR offers innovative approaches to learning. [Mikropoulos & Natsis, 2006] highlights how VR can create experiential learning opportunities that enhance understanding and retention. For instance, medical students can practice surgical procedures in a risk-free environment using VR simulations. Similarly, history students can explore ancient civilizations through immersive experiences that bring the past to life.

3. Healthcare The healthcare sector has embraced VR for therapeutic purposes, particularly in pain management and rehabilitation. Research by [Hoffman et al., 2001] demonstrated that VR can distract patients from pain during medical procedures, leading to reduced discomfort and anxiety. Additionally, VR is used in exposure therapy for conditions such as PTSD, allowing patients to confront their fears in a controlled setting.

4. **Architecture and Design**   Architects and designers utilize VR to visualize projects before construction begins. By creating immersive 3D models, clients can experience spaces in a way that traditional blueprints cannot offer. This application not only enhances client engagement but also facilitates better decision-making during the design process [Miller, 2014].

Challenges and Ethical Considerations

Despite its potential, VR also presents several challenges and ethical concerns:

1. **Accessibility**   One significant issue is the accessibility of VR technology. High costs associated with VR hardware and software can limit its availability to certain demographics, exacerbating the digital divide. [Rogers, 2018] emphasizes the importance of making VR more inclusive to ensure that diverse populations can benefit from its advantages.

2. **Data Privacy and Security**   As VR experiences often require personal data collection, concerns regarding privacy and security arise. Users may unknowingly share sensitive information, leading to potential misuse. [Zuboff, 2019] warns that as VR becomes more integrated into daily life, the need for robust data protection measures will become increasingly critical.

3. **Psychological Effects**   The immersive nature of VR can lead to unintended psychological effects, such as desensitization to violence or addiction to virtual experiences. [Riva, 2016] highlights the need for responsible VR design that considers the potential long-term impacts on users' mental health and social interactions.

Conclusion

In conclusion, Virtual Reality represents a powerful tool with the potential to reshape various aspects of human experience. While its applications in entertainment, education, healthcare, and design are promising, it is essential to address the challenges and ethical considerations that accompany this technology. As VR continues to evolve, it will be crucial for innovators like Kai Ba to navigate these complexities, ensuring that the impact of VR remains positive and inclusive for all.

Bibliography

[Biocca et al., 2001] Biocca, F., Harms, C., & Burgoon, J. K. (2001). Toward a more robust theory and measure of social presence: Review and suggested criteria. *Presence: Teleoperators and Virtual Environments*, 12(5), 456-480.

[Csikszentmihalyi, 1990] Csikszentmihalyi, M. (1990). *Flow: The Psychology of Optimal Experience*. Harper & Row.

[Dixon, 2019] Dixon, M. (2019). The impact of virtual reality on gaming. *Journal of Gaming and Virtual Worlds*, 11(2), 145-160.

[Hoffman et al., 2001] Hoffman, H. G., Patterson, D. R., & Carrougher, G. J. (2001). The effectiveness of virtual reality for pain control in burn wound care: A case study. *Pain*, 92(3), 241-247.

[Mikropoulos & Natsis, 2006] Mikropoulos, T. A., & Natsis, A. (2006). Educational virtual environments: A ten-year review of the research. *Computers & Education*, 46(3), 1-18.

[Miller, 2014] Miller, J. (2014). The role of virtual reality in architecture. *Architectural Design*, 84(2), 78-85.

[Riva, 2016] Riva, G. (2016). Virtual reality in clinical psychology: A review. *Cyberpsychology, Behavior, and Social Networking*, 19(1), 1-6.

[Rogers, 2018] Rogers, Y. (2018). *The Role of Virtual Reality in Promoting Accessibility*. In *The Oxford Handbook of Virtual Reality*.

[Slater & Wilbur, 2009] Slater, M., & Wilbur, S. (2009). A framework for immersive virtual environments (FIVE): Speculations on the role of presence in virtual environments. *Presence: Teleoperators and Virtual Environments*, 8(2), 225-239.

[Zuboff, 2019] Zuboff, S. (2019). *The Age of Surveillance Capitalism: The Fight for a Human Future at the New Frontier of Power*. PublicAffairs.

Exploring Different Cultures

The journey of an innovator is often marked by a rich tapestry of cultural influences that shape their worldview and drive their creativity. For Kai Ba, exploring different cultures was not merely an academic exercise; it was a transformative experience that fueled his passion for technology and innovation. This subsection delves into the significance of cultural exploration in Kai's early life, its impact on his work in holographic environments, and the theoretical frameworks that underpin this exploration.

Cultural Curiosity as a Catalyst for Innovation

From a young age, Kai exhibited a profound curiosity about the world around him. This curiosity was not limited to technology; it extended to the diverse cultures that exist globally. According to the *Cultural Intelligence Theory*, the ability to understand and adapt to different cultural contexts can enhance creativity and problem-solving skills. Kai's exposure to various cultures allowed him to draw inspiration from their unique narratives, traditions, and artistic expressions, which he later integrated into his holographic designs.

$$\text{Cultural Intelligence (CQ)} = \text{Cognitive CQ} + \text{Emotional CQ} + \text{Physical CQ} \quad (1)$$

Where:

- **Cognitive CQ** refers to knowledge of cultural norms and practices.

- **Emotional CQ** involves the ability to empathize and connect with individuals from diverse backgrounds.

- **Physical CQ** denotes the ability to adapt one's behavior in culturally appropriate ways.

Kai's high CQ enabled him to collaborate effectively with a diverse team, fostering an environment of inclusivity and creativity.

Real-World Applications of Cultural Insights

Kai's travels to various countries provided him with firsthand experiences of different cultures. For instance, during a trip to Japan, he was deeply inspired by the concept of *Wabi-Sabi*, which embraces imperfection and transience. This philosophy influenced his approach to designing immersive environments, prompting him to create spaces that celebrated the beauty of imperfection rather than striving for unattainable perfection. He integrated natural elements and organic forms into his holographic worlds, allowing users to experience a sense of serenity and connection to nature.

Moreover, his exposure to African storytelling traditions led him to incorporate narrative techniques into his holographic experiences. By weaving cultural narratives into the design of immersive environments, Kai created a platform that not only entertained but also educated users about different cultures. This approach aligns with the *Cultural Storytelling Framework*, which posits that stories can bridge cultural gaps and foster understanding.

$$\text{Cultural Storytelling} = \text{Narrative} + \text{Cultural Context} + \text{Audience Engagement} \tag{2}$$

Where:

- **Narrative** refers to the story being told.
- **Cultural Context** provides the background that informs the story.
- **Audience Engagement** ensures that the audience connects with the story on a personal level.

Challenges in Cultural Exploration

Despite the benefits of exploring different cultures, Kai faced several challenges. One significant issue was the risk of cultural appropriation, where elements of one culture are borrowed without understanding their significance. To mitigate this risk, Kai adopted a practice of *Cultural Collaboration*, ensuring that he worked closely with cultural representatives when integrating their elements into his projects. This approach not only respected the source cultures but also enriched his work with authenticity and depth.

Furthermore, the challenge of balancing global and local perspectives became evident in his projects. The *Globalization Theory* suggests that while cultures may influence each other, local traditions must be preserved. Kai navigated this complexity by creating customizable holographic experiences that allowed users to choose elements reflective of their cultural backgrounds, thus promoting a sense of ownership and pride.

Examples of Cultural Integration in Holographic Worlds

Kai's commitment to cultural exploration culminated in several groundbreaking projects. One notable example is the *HoloCulture* platform, which allows users to immerse themselves in various cultural experiences. Users can explore the vibrant streets of Rio de Janeiro during Carnival, participate in a traditional tea ceremony in China, or engage in storytelling sessions with Indigenous communities in North America. Each experience is designed to be authentic, drawing on cultural consultants to ensure accuracy and respect.

In another project, Kai collaborated with artists from different cultures to create a series of holographic art installations that celebrate cultural diversity. These installations not only showcased the beauty of various artistic traditions but also served as a platform for dialogue about cultural identity and representation.

Conclusion

In summary, exploring different cultures was a pivotal aspect of Kai Ba's journey as an innovator. His experiences fostered a deep appreciation for diversity and informed his approach to technology and design. By integrating cultural insights into his holographic environments, Kai not only enhanced the user experience but also contributed to a greater understanding of the world's rich tapestry of cultures. As we move forward into an increasingly globalized society, the lessons learned from Kai's exploration of cultures will undoubtedly serve as a guiding light for future innovators.

Education and Formative Experiences

Discovering a Passion for Technology

The journey of discovering a passion for technology is often a multifaceted experience, shaped by personal interests, societal influences, and the inexorable march of innovation. For Kai Ba, this journey began in the early years of his life, where a confluence of curiosity, exposure, and opportunity ignited a fervent interest in the technological realm.

The Spark of Curiosity

From an early age, Kai exhibited an insatiable curiosity about the world around him. This curiosity was not merely a passive observation; it was an active engagement with the mechanics of his environment. Whether it was dismantling household gadgets to understand their inner workings or experimenting with rudimentary coding on his first computer, Kai's hands-on approach laid the groundwork for his future endeavors in technology.

$$C = \frac{I}{E} \quad (3)$$

In this equation, C represents curiosity, I symbolizes the level of interest, and E denotes the exposure to technology. As Kai's exposure increased through books, documentaries, and interactive experiences, his curiosity burgeoned, propelling him toward a deeper understanding of technological principles.

Influences of Family and Community

The familial environment played a crucial role in shaping Kai's passion. His parents, both educators, fostered a culture of inquiry and exploration. They encouraged him to ask questions and seek answers, emphasizing the importance of knowledge and critical thinking. This nurturing environment was complemented by a community that valued innovation and creativity.

"The greatest gift you can give your child is the gift of curiosity."

This sentiment resonated deeply with Kai, as he recognized that his passion for technology was not solely an individual pursuit but a collective journey supported by those around him.

The Role of Education

As Kai progressed through his education, he encountered various subjects that ignited his interest further. Mathematics and physics, in particular, provided the foundational skills necessary for understanding complex technological concepts. The interplay between theoretical knowledge and practical application became evident during his high school years, where he participated in robotics competitions.

$$F = ma \quad (4)$$

In this fundamental equation of motion, F represents force, m is mass, and a is acceleration. Kai applied this principle when designing and programming robots, learning not only the mechanics behind motion but also the importance of precision and creativity in problem-solving.

Experiences with Technology

Kai's first significant experience with technology came when he participated in a summer coding camp. Here, he was introduced to programming languages such as Python and Java. The exhilaration of creating a functional program from scratch was transformative.

> "It was like magic—turning lines of code into something that could interact with the world. I knew then that technology was my path."

This experience solidified his desire to delve deeper into the world of technology, prompting him to seek out additional opportunities for learning and growth.

Exploring the Digital Frontier

As the internet became more prevalent, Kai found himself drawn to online communities that shared his passion for technology. Platforms like GitHub allowed him to collaborate on projects, learn from others, and contribute to open-source initiatives. This sense of community was pivotal in reinforcing his belief that technology was not just a field of study but a collaborative endeavor that could drive societal change.

$$T = \frac{C}{R} \qquad (5)$$

In this equation, T represents technological advancement, C is creativity, and R denotes resources. Kai understood that creativity, when combined with the right resources, could lead to groundbreaking innovations. This realization motivated him to pursue further education in computer science and engineering, where he could harness his creativity and apply it to real-world challenges.

Challenges and Resilience

However, the path to discovering a passion for technology was not without its challenges. Kai faced moments of self-doubt, particularly during rigorous academic pursuits and competitive environments. Yet, these challenges served as critical learning experiences that fostered resilience.

"Every setback was a lesson. I learned to embrace failure as a stepping stone to success."

This mindset proved invaluable as he navigated the complexities of technology, ultimately shaping his approach to innovation.

Conclusion

In conclusion, Kai Ba's discovery of a passion for technology was a multifaceted journey influenced by curiosity, family support, educational experiences, community engagement, and resilience in the face of challenges. This foundation not only set the stage for his future innovations but also instilled a lifelong commitment to exploring the possibilities of technology in shaping a better world. As he moved forward, this passion would become the driving force behind his groundbreaking work in immersive environments, ultimately transforming the way humanity interacts with technology.

Groundbreaking Research Projects

Throughout Kai Ba's academic journey, he engaged in several groundbreaking research projects that not only advanced the field of immersive environments but also showcased the potential of holography and virtual reality in various applications. This subsection delves into the critical research projects that shaped his understanding and expertise, highlighting the theories, challenges, and innovative solutions that emerged.

The Holo-Space Project

One of the first major projects Kai Ba undertook was the Holo-Space Project, which aimed to create a fully immersive virtual environment simulating outer space. This project was built on the theoretical framework of *Spatial Presence Theory*, which posits that the sense of being in a virtual environment can significantly enhance user engagement and learning outcomes.

The Holo-Space Project faced several challenges, including the need for high-fidelity graphics and real-time rendering capabilities. To address these issues, Kai and his team utilized advanced rendering techniques such as *ray tracing* and *level of detail (LOD)* algorithms to optimize performance. The resulting platform allowed users to explore celestial bodies, conduct virtual experiments, and even participate in simulated space missions, providing an unprecedented educational tool for aspiring astronomers.

$$\text{Ray Tracing Time} = \frac{N \cdot D}{R} \qquad (6)$$

where N is the number of rays, D is the depth of the scene, and R is the rendering efficiency.

The Virtual Culture Initiative

In another landmark project, the Virtual Culture Initiative sought to explore the integration of holographic technology with cultural heritage preservation. This project was inspired by the *Cultural Memory Theory*, which emphasizes the importance of preserving cultural artifacts and narratives for future generations.

The initiative involved creating holographic reconstructions of historical sites, allowing users to experience and interact with these environments as they once were. However, challenges arose in accurately capturing the essence of these sites, particularly in terms of scale and detail. To overcome this, Kai's team employed *photogrammetry* techniques, combining thousands of photographs to create 3D models with remarkable fidelity.

$$\text{3D Model Accuracy} = \frac{P \cdot R}{S} \qquad (7)$$

where P is the number of photographs, R is the resolution of each image, and S is the scale of the model.

The project not only provided an innovative way to engage with history but also raised questions about the ethical implications of virtual representations of cultural heritage, leading to discussions on authenticity and representation.

The Mixed Reality Learning Platform

The Mixed Reality Learning Platform was another significant research endeavor that focused on enhancing educational experiences through the integration of augmented and virtual reality. Grounded in *Constructivist Learning Theory*, which posits that knowledge is constructed through interaction with the environment, this project aimed to create a collaborative learning space where students could engage with complex concepts in a hands-on manner.

One of the primary challenges faced was the need for seamless interaction between virtual and physical elements. To tackle this, Kai's team developed a novel *marker-based tracking system* that allowed real-world objects to interact with virtual representations. This system utilized computer vision algorithms to accurately track the position and orientation of physical objects in real time.

$$\text{Tracking Accuracy} = \frac{D_{\text{actual}} - D_{\text{measured}}}{D_{\text{actual}}} \quad (8)$$

where D_{actual} is the actual distance and D_{measured} is the distance measured by the tracking system.

The platform was successfully implemented in various educational settings, demonstrating significant improvements in student engagement and comprehension, particularly in subjects like physics and biology.

The HoloHealth Initiative

Recognizing the potential of holographic technology in healthcare, the HoloHealth Initiative was launched to explore its applications in medical training and patient care. This project drew on *Experiential Learning Theory*, which emphasizes learning through experience and reflection.

The initiative involved creating realistic holographic simulations for surgical training, allowing medical students to practice procedures in a risk-free environment. However, challenges related to the realism of the simulations arose. To enhance the experience, Kai's team collaborated with medical professionals to incorporate real-time feedback mechanisms into the simulations, using *biofeedback* techniques to simulate physiological responses during procedures.

$$\text{Simulation Fidelity} = \frac{R_{\text{feedback}} \cdot A_{\text{realism}}}{C_{\text{complexity}}} \quad (9)$$

where R_{feedback} is the responsiveness of the feedback system, A_{realism} is the level of realism in the simulation, and $C_{\text{complexity}}$ is the complexity of the surgical procedure.

The HoloHealth Initiative not only improved the training of medical professionals but also facilitated better patient understanding of procedures through interactive holographic presentations, ultimately enhancing patient care.

The Eco-Holo Project

The Eco-Holo Project was an ambitious research initiative aimed at using holographic technology to promote environmental awareness and sustainability. Grounded in *Ecological Systems Theory*, which emphasizes the interconnectedness of human and environmental systems, this project sought to visualize the impact of human activities on ecosystems.

One of the significant challenges was creating accurate environmental models that could simulate various scenarios, such as climate change and deforestation. To achieve this, Kai's team developed a comprehensive *environmental simulation engine* that integrated real-time data from environmental sensors and satellite imagery.

$$\text{Ecosystem Impact} = \frac{H_{\text{human}} \cdot E_{\text{environment}}}{I_{\text{intervention}}} \qquad (10)$$

where H_{human} is the human impact factor, $E_{\text{environment}}$ is the environmental resilience factor, and $I_{\text{intervention}}$ is the intervention index.

The Eco-Holo Project successfully engaged communities in environmental conservation efforts, providing immersive experiences that illustrated the consequences of environmental degradation and the importance of sustainable practices.

In conclusion, the groundbreaking research projects undertaken by Kai Ba not only advanced the field of holography and immersive environments but also demonstrated the transformative potential of technology across various domains. Each project faced unique challenges and required innovative solutions, ultimately contributing to the development of a more connected and informed society.

Cross-disciplinary Collaborations

In the rapidly evolving landscape of technology and innovation, cross-disciplinary collaborations have become pivotal in fostering groundbreaking advancements. For Kai Ba, these collaborations were not merely a means to an end; they were the bedrock upon which the Holographic Worlds platform was built. This section explores the significance, challenges, and outcomes of such collaborations in the context of immersive environments.

The Importance of Cross-disciplinary Collaborations

Cross-disciplinary collaborations bring together experts from various fields to tackle complex problems that cannot be solved by a single discipline alone. In the case of Holographic Worlds, Kai Ba recognized early on that the intersection of technology, psychology, art, and ethics was essential for creating truly immersive experiences. The synergy of diverse perspectives leads to innovative solutions and fosters creativity, which is crucial in a field that thrives on imagination.

Theoretical Framework

The theoretical framework underpinning cross-disciplinary collaborations can be understood through the lens of *Complex Adaptive Systems* (CAS). CAS theory posits that systems composed of interconnected elements can adapt and evolve in response to their environment. In the context of Holographic Worlds, each discipline—be it computer science, cognitive psychology, or design—represents an element within the system. The interactions among these elements lead to emergent properties, such as enhanced user experience and ethical considerations in design.

$$\text{Emergence} = f(\text{Interdisciplinary Interactions}) \qquad (11)$$

This equation suggests that the degree of emergence in innovation is a function of the quality and quantity of interdisciplinary interactions.

Challenges in Collaboration

Despite the clear advantages, cross-disciplinary collaborations are fraught with challenges. One significant issue is the *communication barrier* that arises from differing terminologies and methodologies. For instance, a computer scientist may prioritize algorithm efficiency, while a psychologist may focus on user experience. These divergent priorities can lead to misunderstandings and hinder progress.

Moreover, *cultural differences* among disciplines can also pose challenges. Each field has its own norms, values, and practices, which can create friction in collaborative efforts. Kai Ba often navigated these challenges by fostering an inclusive environment where all voices were heard, ensuring that every discipline felt valued in the collaborative process.

Examples of Successful Collaborations

One of the most notable examples of cross-disciplinary collaboration in the development of Holographic Worlds was the partnership with cognitive psychologists. This collaboration aimed to understand how users interact with virtual environments and how these interactions can be optimized for better engagement. The psychologists conducted studies on user behavior, which informed the design of more intuitive interfaces.

Additionally, collaborations with artists and designers played a crucial role in creating aesthetically pleasing and immersive environments. For instance, a partnership with a team of visual artists led to the development of stunning holographic landscapes that enhanced the overall user experience. The integration of art into technology not only made the environments more engaging but also elevated the emotional impact of the experiences.

Case Study: The HoloHealth Project

A prime example of effective cross-disciplinary collaboration was the *HoloHealth Project*, which aimed to revolutionize healthcare training through immersive environments. This project brought together medical professionals, software developers, and educators.

The medical professionals provided insights into the specific skills and scenarios that needed to be simulated, while the software developers worked on creating realistic holographic representations of medical procedures. Educators contributed by designing curricula that integrated the holographic simulations into existing training programs.

The outcome was a comprehensive training module that allowed medical students to practice surgeries in a risk-free environment, significantly improving their confidence and competence. The success of the HoloHealth Project underscored the power of cross-disciplinary collaboration in driving innovation.

Conclusion

In conclusion, cross-disciplinary collaborations were fundamental to the success of Kai Ba's vision for Holographic Worlds. By integrating diverse perspectives and expertise, these collaborations not only enhanced the technological capabilities of the platform but also ensured that ethical considerations were woven into the fabric of immersive experiences. As the field of immersive environments continues to evolve, fostering such collaborations will be essential for addressing the complex challenges that lie ahead.

$$\text{Innovation} = \sum_{i=1}^{n} \text{Expertise}_i \cdot \text{Collaboration Factor} \quad (12)$$

This equation illustrates that innovation is the sum of the expertise from various disciplines, multiplied by the effectiveness of their collaboration. Thus, the future of immersive environments will depend heavily on the ability to cultivate and sustain cross-disciplinary partnerships.

Challenges and Breakthroughs

The journey of innovation is seldom a straight path; it is often marked by numerous challenges that require resilience, creativity, and a willingness to adapt. For Kai Ba, the formative years of his education were riddled with obstacles that tested his commitment to technology and immersive environments. This subsection explores the significant challenges he faced and the breakthroughs that emerged from these experiences.

Theoretical Framework of Innovation Challenges

To understand the nature of challenges faced by innovators, we can reference the *Innovation Diffusion Theory*, which explains how, why, and at what rate new ideas and technology spread. According to Rogers (2003), the adoption of innovations is influenced by five factors: relative advantage, compatibility, complexity, trialability, and observability. Kai Ba's work in holography encountered challenges in these areas, particularly in complexity and compatibility with existing technologies.

Identifying Challenges

1. Technological Complexity One of the foremost challenges Kai encountered was the inherent complexity of developing holographic systems. The intricacies involved in creating realistic and interactive holograms required advanced knowledge in optics, computer science, and engineering. This complexity often led to frustration among team members, as the learning curve was steep.

2. Resource Limitations Financial constraints posed another significant hurdle. In the early stages of his research, securing funding was a constant battle. Many investors were skeptical about the feasibility and marketability of holographic technology. This skepticism was rooted in the historical challenges of virtual reality, which had seen several cycles of hype and disappointment.

3. Interdisciplinary Collaboration While cross-disciplinary collaboration is essential for innovation, it also presents challenges. Kai's vision required expertise from various fields, including psychology, design, and engineering. Coordinating between these disciplines often resulted in miscommunication and conflicting priorities, complicating project timelines and outcomes.

4. Ethical Concerns As Kai delved deeper into immersive environments, ethical concerns regarding privacy, data security, and the psychological impact of prolonged virtual interactions emerged. These concerns were not only technical but also philosophical, as they questioned the implications of creating experiences that could blur the lines between reality and illusion.

Breakthroughs Arising from Challenges

Despite the obstacles, each challenge led to significant breakthroughs that shaped Kai's innovative journey.

1. Simplifying Technology To address technological complexity, Kai initiated a series of workshops focused on simplifying the underlying technology. By breaking down complex concepts into digestible modules, he empowered his team to tackle specific components of the holographic system. This approach not only enhanced team understanding but also fostered a culture of collaborative problem-solving.

2. Innovative Funding Solutions In response to resource limitations, Kai explored unconventional funding avenues, such as crowdfunding and partnerships with educational institutions. This strategy not only secured necessary resources but also engaged a community of supporters who became advocates for the technology. The success of a crowdfunding campaign demonstrated public interest in holographic technology, attracting further investments.

3. Enhancing Interdisciplinary Communication To mitigate collaboration issues, Kai implemented regular interdisciplinary meetings, establishing a shared language and common goals. By fostering an environment of open communication, team members were encouraged to voice concerns and share insights, leading to innovative solutions that integrated diverse perspectives.

4. Addressing Ethical Concerns Proactively Recognizing the importance of ethical considerations, Kai established an ethics committee within his lab. This committee was tasked with evaluating the implications of their work, ensuring that ethical standards were integrated into the development process. By prioritizing ethics, Kai not only addressed concerns but also positioned his work as responsible and forward-thinking.

Case Study: The HoloHealth Initiative

A notable example of overcoming challenges is the *HoloHealth Initiative*, a project aimed at utilizing holographic technology for medical training. Initially met with skepticism regarding its practicality and effectiveness, the project faced significant hurdles in acceptance within the medical community.

1. **Challenge: Skepticism in Medical Training** Medical professionals were hesitant to embrace holographic simulations, doubting their ability to replicate real-life scenarios effectively.

2. **Breakthrough: Pilot Programs** In response, Kai organized pilot programs that allowed medical students to experience holographic training firsthand. Feedback from these sessions highlighted the advantages of immersive learning, such as improved retention and engagement. The positive outcomes from these pilots led to wider acceptance and integration of holographic training in medical curricula.

Conclusion

The challenges faced by Kai Ba during his educational journey were not mere obstacles but catalysts for innovation. Each difficulty prompted creative solutions and breakthroughs that ultimately contributed to the evolution of holographic technology. By embracing challenges and transforming them into opportunities, Kai not only advanced his work but also set a precedent for future innovators in the field of immersive environments.

Mentorship and Guidance

Mentorship plays a crucial role in shaping the trajectory of an innovator's career, particularly in the rapidly evolving field of technology. For Kai Ba, mentorship was not merely a guiding force but a foundational pillar that supported his journey into the realm of immersive environments. This section explores the multifaceted nature of mentorship in Kai's life, its theoretical underpinnings, and its practical implications in fostering innovation.

Theoretical Framework of Mentorship

Mentorship can be understood through various theoretical lenses. One prominent theory is the *Social Learning Theory* proposed by Albert Bandura, which emphasizes the importance of observational learning, imitation, and modeling. According to Bandura, individuals learn not only through direct experience but also by observing others, particularly those they admire or consider role models. In the context of Kai Ba, his mentors served as exemplars of success, demonstrating not only technical skills but also the ethical considerations and emotional resilience required in the tech industry.

Moreover, the *Transformational Leadership Theory* highlights the impact of mentors who inspire and motivate their mentees to exceed their own expectations. Mentors in Kai's life were not just advisors; they were catalysts for change, encouraging him to explore uncharted territories and embrace challenges. This transformative relationship often leads to increased self-efficacy among mentees, enabling them to tackle complex problems with confidence.

The Role of Mentorship in Kai Ba's Development

Kai's early exposure to technology was significantly influenced by mentors who recognized his potential. One of the pivotal figures was Dr. Lila Chen, a pioneer in virtual reality research. Dr. Chen provided Kai with access to cutting-edge research opportunities, guiding him through complex projects that would eventually lay the groundwork for his later innovations. Her mentorship was characterized by a hands-on approach, allowing Kai to engage directly with technology while fostering critical thinking.

In addition to technical guidance, Dr. Chen emphasized the importance of interdisciplinary collaboration. She often quoted the adage, "Great innovations arise at the intersection of disciplines," encouraging Kai to seek insights from fields such as psychology, art, and sociology. This holistic perspective not only enriched his understanding of technology but also sparked the idea of creating immersive environments that resonate with users on multiple levels.

Challenges Faced in Mentorship Relationships

Despite the benefits, mentorship relationships can also present challenges. One common issue is the potential for dependency, where mentees may become overly reliant on their mentors for guidance. This can stifle creativity and inhibit independent problem-solving skills. Kai experienced this firsthand when he found himself struggling to make decisions without consulting Dr. Chen. Recognizing this pattern, he sought to cultivate his autonomy by setting personal goals and embracing failure as a learning opportunity.

Another challenge is the potential for mismatched expectations between mentors and mentees. In some cases, mentors may have a vision for their mentees that does not align with the mentee's aspirations. For instance, while Dr. Chen envisioned Kai as a leader in academic research, Kai's passion lay in applying technology for social impact. Open communication became crucial in navigating this discrepancy, leading to a mutual understanding that allowed Kai to forge his own path while still benefiting from Dr. Chen's wisdom.

Examples of Successful Mentorship in Innovation

Several notable examples illustrate the profound impact of mentorship on innovation. Steve Jobs, co-founder of Apple Inc., often credited his mentor, Robert Friedland, with shaping his entrepreneurial spirit and design philosophy. Friedland encouraged Jobs to explore the intersection of technology and the humanities, a principle that became central to Apple's innovative products.

Similarly, Kai Ba's mentorship experiences mirrored these success stories. His collaboration with industry leaders and academics resulted in groundbreaking projects that transformed the landscape of immersive environments. One such project was the development of a holographic interface for medical training, which emerged from a mentorship-driven initiative that brought together experts from healthcare, technology, and education.

Conclusion: The Lasting Impact of Mentorship

In conclusion, mentorship is a vital component of personal and professional growth, particularly in fields characterized by rapid change and complexity. For Kai Ba, the guidance he received from mentors like Dr. Lila Chen not only shaped his technical abilities but also instilled a sense of ethical responsibility and a commitment to innovation. As Kai continues to inspire the next generation of innovators, the lessons learned from his mentors remain a testament to the transformative power of mentorship in fostering creativity and resilience.

The journey of mentorship is ongoing, and as Kai Ba reflects on his experiences, he emphasizes the importance of giving back. He actively engages in mentorship programs, believing that by nurturing the next wave of innovators, he can contribute to a future where technology serves humanity in profound and meaningful ways. The cycle of mentorship continues, proving that the guidance of one can illuminate the path for many.

Enter the World of Immersion

Exploring the Potential of Holography

Holography, a technique that enables the recording and reconstruction of light fields, has emerged as a transformative technology with vast potential across various sectors. At its core, holography relies on the principles of interference and diffraction of light, allowing for the creation of three-dimensional images that can be viewed without the need for special glasses. This section delves into the theoretical underpinnings of holography, its practical applications, and the challenges that accompany its implementation.

Theoretical Foundations

The fundamental principle of holography involves the interference of coherent light waves, typically produced by a laser. When a laser beam is split into two paths—one directed onto the object and the other onto a recording medium—an interference pattern is created. This pattern encodes both the amplitude and phase information of the light waves reflected from the object, resulting in a hologram. The mathematical representation of this process can be described using the wavefronts of light, represented as:

$$E(x, y, z) = A(x, y)e^{i\phi(x,y,z)} \qquad (13)$$

where E is the electric field of the light wave, A is the amplitude, and ϕ is the phase. The hologram can then be reconstructed by illuminating it with coherent light, resulting in a three-dimensional image that appears to float in space.

Applications of Holography

The potential applications of holography are vast and varied, impacting fields such as healthcare, education, entertainment, and security.

Healthcare In the medical field, holography has been utilized for advanced imaging techniques. For instance, holographic imaging can be employed to visualize complex anatomical structures in three dimensions, enhancing the precision of surgical procedures. A notable example is the use of holographic displays to project 3D models of organs derived from MRI and CT scans, allowing surgeons to better plan operations. The ability to manipulate these holograms in real-time can significantly reduce the risks associated with invasive procedures.

Education Holography also holds immense promise in educational settings. By creating immersive learning environments, students can engage with complex concepts in a more tangible manner. For example, a holographic model of the solar system can provide an interactive experience for students studying astronomy, allowing them to explore planetary movements and spatial relationships in a way that textbooks cannot offer.

Entertainment   In the realm of entertainment, holography has the potential to revolutionize how audiences experience performances. Holographic concerts, where deceased artists appear as lifelike projections, have already begun to captivate audiences. Moreover, holographic gaming experiences can transport players into fantastical worlds, enhancing the interactivity and immersion of gameplay.

Security   Holography is also employed in security applications, particularly in anti-counterfeiting measures. Holograms on credit cards, passports, and product packaging serve as a deterrent against forgery due to their complex and difficult-to-reproduce nature. The unique properties of holograms make them an effective tool for ensuring the authenticity of valuable items.

Challenges and Limitations

Despite its potential, several challenges and limitations hinder the widespread adoption of holography.

Technical Limitations   One significant hurdle is the complexity of holographic systems. The equipment required for high-quality holography, such as lasers and specialized recording media, can be expensive and difficult to operate. Additionally, the resolution of holograms is often limited by the recording medium's sensitivity and the coherence length of the laser used, which can restrict the detail captured in the holographic image.

Perception and Accessibility   Another challenge lies in the perception and accessibility of holographic displays. While holography can create stunning visuals, the technology is still in its infancy regarding user-friendly interfaces. Current holographic displays often require specific viewing angles and conditions to be effective, which can limit their practicality in everyday applications.

Ethical Considerations   Finally, ethical considerations surrounding holography must be addressed. The ability to create realistic representations of individuals raises concerns regarding consent and privacy. For instance, the use of holograms to recreate deceased individuals for entertainment purposes can be seen as controversial, prompting discussions about the moral implications of such technologies.

Conclusion

In conclusion, holography represents a frontier of innovation with the potential to reshape numerous industries. While the theoretical foundations of holography are well-established, the practical applications continue to evolve, presenting exciting opportunities and formidable challenges. As researchers and innovators like Kai Ba explore the possibilities of holographic technology, the journey towards realizing its full potential is just beginning. As we stand on the cusp of this new era, it is imperative to navigate the technical, ethical, and societal implications that accompany such a transformative medium.

Developments in Augmented Reality

Augmented Reality (AR) has emerged as a transformative technology that overlays digital information onto the real world, enhancing the user's perception and interaction with their environment. This subsection explores the theoretical foundations, recent advancements, challenges, and practical applications of AR.

Theoretical Foundations of Augmented Reality

At its core, AR combines the physical and digital worlds through the integration of computer-generated images, sounds, and other sensory stimuli. The theoretical framework for AR can be understood through the following components:

1. **Computer Vision:** This field enables machines to interpret and understand visual information from the world. By using algorithms that analyze images and videos, AR systems can recognize objects, track their movements, and overlay relevant digital content.

2. **User Interaction:** AR systems must be designed with user interaction in mind, employing intuitive interfaces that allow users to manipulate digital content seamlessly. Theories of human-computer interaction (HCI) guide the design of these systems, focusing on usability and user experience.

3. **Context Awareness:** AR applications often rely on contextual information to provide relevant content. Context-aware computing involves utilizing sensors and data analytics to understand the user's environment, preferences, and behaviors.

Recent Advancements in Augmented Reality

The field of AR has witnessed significant developments in recent years, driven by advancements in hardware, software, and algorithms. Key areas of progress include:

1. **Mobile AR:** The proliferation of smartphones equipped with powerful processors, cameras, and sensors has made mobile AR accessible to a broader audience. Applications like *Pokémon GO* and *IKEA Place* have demonstrated the potential of mobile AR in gaming and interior design, respectively.
2. **Wearable AR Devices:** Devices such as Microsoft HoloLens and Magic Leap have pushed the boundaries of AR by providing immersive experiences through head-mounted displays. These devices utilize advanced sensors and spatial mapping technologies to create realistic interactions between digital and physical objects.
3. **Cloud-Based AR:** Cloud computing has enabled the development of AR applications that require extensive processing power and storage capabilities. By offloading computations to the cloud, developers can create more complex and data-rich AR experiences.
4. **Artificial Intelligence Integration:** The integration of AI into AR systems has enhanced object recognition, scene understanding, and user interaction. Machine learning algorithms allow AR applications to adapt to user behaviors and preferences, creating personalized experiences.

Challenges in Augmented Reality Development

Despite the rapid advancements in AR technology, several challenges remain:
1. **Technical Limitations:** Current AR systems often struggle with issues such as latency, tracking inaccuracies, and limited field of view. These limitations can hinder the user experience and lead to disorientation or frustration.
2. **Content Creation:** Developing high-quality AR content requires specialized skills and tools. The lack of standardized platforms for content creation can lead to fragmentation in the AR ecosystem.
3. **Privacy and Security:** AR applications often rely on user data to provide personalized experiences, raising concerns about privacy and data security. Developers must implement robust measures to protect user information and comply with regulations.
4. **User Acceptance:** While AR has gained popularity, some users remain skeptical about its practicality and safety. Building trust and demonstrating the value of AR applications are crucial for widespread adoption.

Examples of Augmented Reality Applications

AR technology has found applications across various industries, showcasing its versatility and potential impact:

1. **Healthcare:** AR is revolutionizing medical training and surgical procedures. For instance, *AccuVein* uses AR to visualize veins on a patient's skin, aiding healthcare professionals in venipuncture.

2. **Education:** AR enhances learning experiences by providing interactive and immersive content. Applications like *Google Expeditions* allow students to explore historical sites and scientific concepts in a virtual environment.

3. **Retail:** Retailers are leveraging AR to improve customer engagement. For example, *Sephora's Virtual Artist* allows users to try on makeup virtually, enhancing the shopping experience.

4. **Manufacturing and Maintenance:** AR assists technicians in complex assembly and maintenance tasks by overlaying instructions and schematics onto physical equipment. Companies like *Boeing* have implemented AR for wiring harness assembly, resulting in increased efficiency and reduced errors.

5. **Tourism and Navigation:** AR applications enhance travel experiences by providing real-time information about landmarks and attractions. For instance, *Google Lens* can identify objects and provide contextual information, enriching the user's exploration.

In conclusion, the developments in Augmented Reality have the potential to reshape various sectors by enhancing human interaction with digital content. As technology continues to evolve, addressing the challenges of AR will be essential for unlocking its full potential and ensuring its responsible use in society.

Breaking Barriers with Mixed Reality

Mixed Reality (MR) represents a transformative frontier in the realm of immersive technologies, effectively merging the digital and physical worlds to create interactive environments that respond to user actions in real-time. This subsection explores the theoretical foundations, practical applications, challenges, and future potential of Mixed Reality, exemplifying how it breaks barriers across various sectors.

Theoretical Foundations

Mixed Reality exists on a continuum between the real and virtual environments, as illustrated in Figure ??. This continuum ranges from Augmented Reality (AR), which overlays digital information onto the real world, to Virtual Reality (VR), which immerses users in entirely digital spaces. Mixed Reality, however, allows for interactions between real and virtual objects, enabling users to manipulate both environments simultaneously.

$$MR = f(AR, VR) \qquad (14)$$

Where: - MR represents Mixed Reality, - AR is Augmented Reality, - VR is Virtual Reality.

The essence of MR lies in its ability to anchor virtual objects in the real world, allowing for a seamless blend of both domains. This is achieved through advanced tracking technologies and spatial mapping, which recognize physical spaces and adjust virtual content accordingly.

Applications of Mixed Reality

Mixed Reality has found applications in numerous fields, demonstrating its versatility and potential to revolutionize traditional practices:

- **Healthcare:** MR is transforming medical training and patient care. For instance, the Microsoft HoloLens is utilized in surgical simulations, allowing medical students to practice procedures in a risk-free environment. Surgeons can visualize internal organs in 3D, enhancing their understanding of complex anatomies.

- **Education:** MR can create immersive learning experiences that engage students in ways traditional methods cannot. For example, platforms like zSpace allow students to explore the human body or historical events interactively, fostering deeper understanding and retention of knowledge.

- **Architecture and Design:** Architects use MR to visualize their projects in situ, allowing clients to experience a building before it is constructed. Tools like the HoloLens enable architects to overlay digital models onto physical spaces, facilitating real-time modifications based on client feedback.

- **Entertainment and Gaming:** MR is reshaping the gaming landscape by blending gameplay with the physical environment. Games like Pokémon GO have demonstrated the potential of MR to engage users in outdoor spaces, creating a novel form of interactive entertainment that encourages physical activity.

Challenges in Mixed Reality Development

Despite its promise, the development of Mixed Reality technologies is fraught with challenges:

- **Technical Limitations:** Accurate spatial mapping and object recognition remain significant hurdles. The technology must be able to distinguish between various surfaces and objects in real-time, which is computationally intensive and requires advanced sensors.

- **User Experience:** Designing intuitive user interfaces for MR applications is critical. Users must be able to interact with both digital and physical elements seamlessly, which necessitates extensive user testing and iterative design processes.

- **Cost and Accessibility:** The high cost of MR hardware can limit its adoption, particularly in education and healthcare settings. Ensuring that these technologies are affordable and accessible is vital for widespread implementation.

Case Studies: Breaking Barriers

Several case studies illustrate how Mixed Reality is breaking barriers in various sectors:

- **Case Study 1: HoloAnatomy** - Developed by Case Western Reserve University, HoloAnatomy utilizes MR to teach anatomy. Medical students can interact with 3D holograms of human anatomy, significantly enhancing their learning experience compared to traditional textbooks.

- **Case Study 2: The Mixed Reality Lab at the University of Southern California** - This lab focuses on the integration of MR in collaborative design processes. By allowing teams to visualize and manipulate 3D models in real-time, MR fosters creativity and innovation in product development.

- **Case Study 3: Boeing's Use of MR in Manufacturing** - Boeing employs MR to assist engineers in assembly processes. By overlaying digital instructions onto physical components, workers can reduce assembly time and errors, illustrating MR's potential to enhance productivity in manufacturing.

Future Directions

The future of Mixed Reality is promising, with several emerging trends that could further enhance its impact:

- **Advancements in AI and Machine Learning:** The integration of AI can improve object recognition and spatial mapping, making MR experiences more fluid and responsive.

- **Increased Collaboration:** As MR technology becomes more refined, it could facilitate remote collaboration in real-time, allowing teams to work together across distances as if they were in the same physical space.

- **Integration with IoT Devices:** The convergence of MR with the Internet of Things (IoT) could lead to smart environments that respond dynamically to user interactions, further blurring the lines between the digital and physical worlds.

In conclusion, Mixed Reality stands at the forefront of technological innovation, breaking barriers across various sectors by enhancing interactivity, engagement, and collaboration. As technology continues to evolve, the potential for MR to reshape our understanding and interaction with the world around us is boundless.

Transforming Industries with Virtual Reality

Virtual Reality (VR) has emerged as a transformative technology across various industries, revolutionizing the way businesses operate, train employees, and engage customers. By immersing users in a digital environment, VR enables experiences that are not only interactive but also highly engaging, leading to enhanced learning, improved efficiency, and innovative solutions to complex problems.

Theoretical Framework of Virtual Reality in Industries

The integration of VR into industry practices can be understood through several theoretical lenses, including experiential learning theory and constructivist learning theory. Experiential learning, as proposed by Kolb (1984), emphasizes the importance of experience in the learning process. VR provides a unique platform for experiential learning, allowing users to engage in simulated environments where they can practice skills and apply knowledge in real-world scenarios without the associated risks.

$$\text{Learning} = f(\text{Experience}, \text{Reflection}, \text{Conceptualization}, \text{Experimentation}) \tag{15}$$

In this equation, learning is a function of the cyclical process involving experience, reflection, conceptualization, and experimentation. VR facilitates this cycle by allowing users to immerse themselves in experiences that require reflection and adaptation.

Industry Applications of Virtual Reality

2.1 Healthcare In the healthcare sector, VR is being utilized for surgical training, patient rehabilitation, and therapeutic interventions. For instance, the use of VR simulations allows medical students to practice surgical techniques in a risk-free environment. A study by Seymour et al. (2002) demonstrated that surgical trainees who practiced in a VR environment showed a significant improvement in their skills compared to those who trained using traditional methods.

2.2 Education and Training In education, VR has transformed traditional classroom settings into immersive learning experiences. Through VR, students can explore historical events, scientific phenomena, or complex mathematical concepts in a three-dimensional space. For example, platforms like Google Expeditions allow students to take virtual field trips to places like the Great Barrier Reef or the surface of Mars, enhancing engagement and retention of information.

2.3 Manufacturing and Engineering In manufacturing, VR is used for design and prototyping, enabling engineers to visualize and manipulate 3D models before physical production. This not only accelerates the design process but also reduces costs associated with prototyping errors. Companies like Ford have implemented VR in their design processes, resulting in a more efficient workflow and improved product quality.

2.4 Real Estate and Architecture The real estate industry has also benefited from VR technology through virtual property tours, allowing potential buyers to explore homes remotely. This capability has become particularly valuable in a global market where physical presence is not always feasible. Similarly, architects use VR to present designs to clients, providing an immersive experience that traditional blueprints cannot achieve.

Challenges in Implementing Virtual Reality

Despite its potential, the adoption of VR in various industries faces several challenges:

3.1 Cost of Implementation The initial investment required for VR technology can be a significant barrier for many organizations. High-quality VR hardware and software can be expensive, and not all companies are willing to allocate resources for such technologies.

3.2 Technical Limitations Technical limitations, such as the need for high-performance computing and potential motion sickness experienced by users, can hinder the effectiveness of VR applications. Ensuring a seamless and comfortable experience is crucial for widespread adoption.

3.3 Resistance to Change Cultural resistance within organizations can also impede the integration of VR. Employees accustomed to traditional methods may be hesitant to adopt new technologies, necessitating comprehensive training and change management strategies.

Future Prospects of Virtual Reality in Industries

As technology continues to advance, the future of VR in industry looks promising. Innovations in hardware, such as lighter headsets and improved graphics, alongside developments in software, including more intuitive user interfaces, are expected to enhance user experiences.

4.1 Integration with Artificial Intelligence The integration of AI with VR can lead to even more personalized and adaptive learning experiences. AI algorithms can analyze user interactions and tailor content to meet individual needs, making VR applications more effective in training and education.

4.2 Expansion into New Sectors New sectors, such as tourism and retail, are beginning to explore VR applications. Virtual tourism experiences allow users to explore destinations without leaving their homes, while retailers are using VR to create immersive shopping experiences that engage customers in novel ways.

Conclusion

In conclusion, Virtual Reality is not merely a technological novelty; it is a powerful tool that has the potential to transform industries. By providing immersive, experiential learning opportunities, enhancing design processes, and revolutionizing customer engagement, VR is paving the way for a future where businesses operate more efficiently and effectively. As organizations continue to embrace this technology, the possibilities for innovation and improvement are limitless.

Ethics and Responsibility in Virtual Reality

The advent of virtual reality (VR) has revolutionized the way we interact with digital content, offering immersive experiences that can enhance learning, entertainment, and social engagement. However, with great power comes great responsibility, and the ethical implications of VR technology must be critically examined. This section explores the ethical considerations and responsibilities that innovators, developers, and users must navigate in the realm of virtual reality.

Ethical Considerations in VR Design

The design of virtual environments raises significant ethical questions regarding user experience and interaction. One critical consideration is the concept of **informed consent**. Users must be fully aware of what they are entering into when they don a VR headset. This includes understanding the potential psychological impacts, data collection practices, and the immersive nature of the experience. Developers have a responsibility to ensure that users are informed and that consent is obtained without coercion.

Psychological Impact and User Well-being

Research indicates that immersive experiences can lead to both positive and negative psychological effects. While VR can be used therapeutically to treat conditions such as PTSD, it can also induce anxiety, disorientation, or even addiction. The **Media Equation Theory**, which posits that people treat media as real social actors, suggests that users may respond emotionally to virtual experiences as if they were real. This phenomenon necessitates that developers consider the emotional and psychological ramifications of their designs.

$$\text{User Impact} = f(\text{Immersion}, \text{Interactivity}, \text{Emotional Response}) \qquad (16)$$

This equation reflects that the user impact is a function of immersion, interactivity, and emotional response, emphasizing the need for balance in creating engaging yet safe virtual environments.

Privacy and Data Security

The collection and use of personal data in VR applications present another ethical challenge. VR systems often require extensive data collection to function effectively, including biometric data, behavioral patterns, and user interactions. Developers must implement robust data protection measures to safeguard user privacy. The **General Data Protection Regulation (GDPR)** provides a framework for data protection, mandating that users have the right to know what data is collected and how it is used.

$$\text{Data Protection} = \frac{\text{Transparency} + \text{User Control}}{\text{Data Collection}} \qquad (17)$$

This equation illustrates that effective data protection relies on transparency and user control over their data in relation to the extent of data collection.

Inclusivity and Accessibility

Ethical VR design must prioritize inclusivity and accessibility to ensure that diverse populations can benefit from these technologies. This includes considering users with disabilities, varying socio-economic backgrounds, and different cultural contexts. The **Universal Design Principles** should be applied to create experiences that are usable by all people, regardless of their abilities or circumstances.

Real-World Consequences of Virtual Actions

The line between virtual and real-world behavior can blur, raising ethical concerns about how users may behave in virtual environments. The **Social Learning Theory** posits that individuals learn behaviors through observation and imitation. Thus, violent or unethical behavior in VR could translate into real-world actions. Developers must take responsibility for the content they create, ensuring that it promotes positive behavior rather than harmful actions.

$$\text{Behavioral Transfer} = \text{Observation} \times \text{Imitation} \qquad (18)$$

This equation highlights the relationship between observation and imitation in behavior transfer, necessitating careful consideration of the content presented in VR.

Ethical Guidelines and Frameworks

In response to these ethical challenges, various organizations and scholars have proposed guidelines for responsible VR development. The **IEEE Global Initiative on Ethics of Autonomous and Intelligent Systems** emphasizes the importance of ethical considerations in design and implementation. The guidelines advocate for transparency, accountability, and fairness in VR applications, encouraging developers to engage with stakeholders and users in the design process.

Conclusion

As VR technology continues to evolve, the ethical responsibilities of innovators and developers will become increasingly complex. By prioritizing informed consent, user well-being, privacy, inclusivity, and the real-world implications of virtual actions, the industry can foster a more responsible approach to virtual reality. The future of VR lies not only in its technological capabilities but also in the ethical frameworks that guide its development and use. It is imperative that all stakeholders engage in ongoing discussions about the ethical implications of their work, ensuring that virtual worlds enhance human experience without compromising ethical standards.

The Revolution Begins

Founding the Immersive Environments Lab

Vision and Mission of the Lab

The Immersive Environments Lab, founded by Kai Ba, is driven by a clear vision: to create a transformative platform that redefines how individuals interact with digital and physical realities. The mission of the lab encompasses several key objectives that align with this vision, aiming to push the boundaries of technology and human experience.

Vision Statement

At its core, the vision of the Immersive Environments Lab is to harness the power of holography and mixed reality to craft environments that are not only immersive but also accessible and equitable. The lab aspires to create virtual experiences that transcend geographical and social barriers, enabling users to connect, learn, and innovate in ways previously thought impossible. This vision is rooted in the belief that technology should serve humanity, enhancing our understanding of the world and fostering collaboration across diverse communities.

Mission Objectives

To achieve this vision, the lab has outlined the following mission objectives:

- **Innovative Research and Development:** The lab is committed to advancing research in holography, augmented reality (AR), and virtual reality (VR). By exploring cutting-edge technologies and methodologies, the lab aims to develop tools and platforms that facilitate immersive experiences across various sectors, including education, healthcare, and entertainment.

- **Interdisciplinary Collaboration:** Recognizing that innovation thrives in diverse environments, the lab actively seeks partnerships with experts from various fields, including computer science, psychology, design, and the arts. This interdisciplinary approach fosters creativity and ensures that the solutions developed are holistic and user-centered.

- **Ethical Framework:** The lab prioritizes ethical considerations in the development of immersive technologies. It aims to address potential issues related to privacy, data security, and the psychological impacts of prolonged exposure to virtual environments. By establishing a robust ethical framework, the lab seeks to ensure that its innovations contribute positively to society.

- **Accessibility and Inclusion:** A key mission of the lab is to make immersive technologies accessible to all individuals, regardless of their background or abilities. This involves designing user interfaces that are intuitive and inclusive, as well as creating content that reflects diverse perspectives and experiences.

- **Education and Empowerment:** The lab is dedicated to empowering users through education. By providing resources, workshops, and training programs, the lab aims to equip individuals with the skills necessary to navigate and contribute to the evolving landscape of immersive environments. This commitment to education extends to advocating for STEM (Science, Technology, Engineering, and Mathematics) initiatives that inspire the next generation of innovators.

Theoretical Foundations

The vision and mission of the Immersive Environments Lab are grounded in several theoretical frameworks that inform its approach to innovation:

Constructivist Learning Theory This theory posits that individuals construct knowledge through experiences and interactions with their environment. The lab's focus on immersive environments aligns with this theory, as it creates spaces where users can engage with content in meaningful ways. For example, a virtual reality simulation of historical events allows users to experience and understand history not just through text but through active participation.

Social Presence Theory Social presence theory emphasizes the importance of feeling connected to others in virtual environments. The lab's mission to foster collaboration and connection through immersive experiences is rooted in this theory. By creating holographic worlds that enable real-time interaction among users, the lab enhances the sense of social presence, making virtual interactions feel more authentic and engaging.

Human-Computer Interaction (HCI) HCI focuses on the design and use of computer technology, emphasizing the interfaces between people (users) and computers. The lab's commitment to creating user-centered designs is informed by HCI principles, ensuring that the technologies developed are intuitive and enhance the user experience.

Examples of Impact

The mission of the Immersive Environments Lab has already begun to show tangible results:

- **Healthcare Innovations:** The lab developed a holographic training program for medical students that simulates complex surgical procedures. This program allows students to practice in a risk-free environment, enhancing their skills and confidence before they enter real operating rooms.

- **Educational Platforms:** In collaboration with educators, the lab created an AR application that brings historical artifacts to life in classrooms. Students can interact with 3D models of ancient civilizations, fostering a deeper understanding of history through immersive learning experiences.

- **Community Engagement:** The lab has initiated outreach programs that provide access to immersive technologies for underrepresented communities. These programs aim to inspire creativity and innovation among youth, encouraging them to explore careers in technology and the arts.

Conclusion

The vision and mission of the Immersive Environments Lab encapsulate a commitment to innovation, collaboration, and ethical responsibility. By striving to create immersive experiences that are accessible, inclusive, and educational, the lab aims to redefine the relationship between technology and humanity. As Kai Ba leads the charge in this endeavor, the lab stands poised to make significant contributions to the future of immersive environments, shaping a world where technology enhances our collective experience and understanding.

Assembling a Dream Team

As Kai Ba embarked on the ambitious journey of founding the Immersive Environments Lab, the first step was to assemble a team that could transform his vision into reality. The process of assembling a dream team is both an art and a science, requiring a careful balance of skills, personalities, and shared values. This section explores the theoretical underpinnings of team dynamics, the challenges faced during the assembly, and the strategies employed to cultivate a high-performing team.

Theoretical Foundations of Team Dynamics

In organizational behavior, the concept of team dynamics refers to the behavioral relationships between members of a team. According to Tuckman's stages of group development, teams typically progress through five stages: forming, storming, norming, performing, and adjourning [Tuckman(1965)]. Understanding these stages is crucial for leaders like Kai Ba, as it provides a framework for navigating the complexities of team interactions.

The forming stage is characterized by initial interactions where team members get to know each other. During this phase, Kai focused on establishing a clear vision and mission for the lab, which would serve as a guiding principle for the team. The storming stage often involves conflicts and competition as individuals assert their ideas and roles. Kai anticipated this phase and prepared to mediate disputes, promoting open communication and encouraging constructive feedback.

Identifying Key Roles and Skills

To build a cohesive team, Kai recognized the importance of identifying key roles and the diverse skills required for the lab's success. Drawing on Belbin's Team Roles theory, he sought individuals who could fill various roles, such as:

- **Plant:** Creative thinkers who generate innovative ideas.
- **Resource Investigator:** Extroverted individuals who explore opportunities and establish contacts.
- **Coordinator:** Individuals who help clarify goals and delegate tasks effectively.

- **Completer-Finisher:** Detail-oriented members who ensure thoroughness and quality.
- **Shaper:** Dynamic individuals who drive the team forward and challenge inertia.

By assembling a team with a balance of these roles, Kai aimed to foster a collaborative environment that would encourage creativity and innovation while maintaining focus on project goals.

Recruitment Strategies

Kai employed a multi-faceted recruitment strategy to attract the right talent. He leveraged his network within academic institutions, industry conferences, and online platforms to identify potential candidates. Moreover, he emphasized the lab's mission to revolutionize immersive environments, which resonated with individuals passionate about technology and its potential to transform society.

To ensure a good fit, Kai implemented a rigorous selection process that included:

1. **Behavioral Interviews:** Focusing on past experiences and problem-solving abilities.
2. **Team-Based Assessments:** Evaluating candidates in group settings to observe interpersonal dynamics.
3. **Skill Assessments:** Testing technical competencies relevant to holography and virtual reality.

This comprehensive approach allowed Kai to assemble a diverse team with complementary skills and shared values, enhancing the lab's collaborative culture.

Fostering a Collaborative Culture

Once the team was assembled, Kai prioritized fostering a collaborative culture. Drawing on Schein's model of organizational culture, he established norms and values that emphasized trust, respect, and open communication [Schein(2010)]. Regular team-building activities and brainstorming sessions were organized to strengthen relationships and encourage creative thinking.

One notable example was a retreat where team members participated in immersive experiences themselves, allowing them to better understand the technology they were developing. This not only built camaraderie but also aligned the team around a shared purpose.

Challenges and Solutions

Despite the initial successes, Kai faced several challenges in maintaining team cohesion. Conflicts arose due to differing opinions on project direction and resource allocation. To address these issues, Kai implemented conflict resolution strategies, including:

- **Open Forums:** Regular meetings where team members could voice concerns and propose solutions.

- **Mediation Techniques:** Facilitating discussions to help members understand differing perspectives.

- **Feedback Mechanisms:** Anonymous surveys to gauge team morale and identify areas for improvement.

These strategies fostered an environment where team members felt valued and heard, ultimately enhancing collaboration and productivity.

Conclusion

Assembling a dream team for the Immersive Environments Lab was a critical step in Kai Ba's journey as an innovator. By leveraging theoretical frameworks, identifying key roles, and fostering a collaborative culture, Kai successfully built a diverse and dynamic team capable of pushing the boundaries of holographic technology. The challenges faced along the way served as valuable learning experiences, reinforcing the importance of adaptability and open communication in team dynamics. The lab's early successes can be attributed not only to the innovative ideas generated but also to the strong foundation of collaboration and mutual respect established by Kai and his team.

Bibliography

[Tuckman(1965)] Tuckman, B.W. (1965). Developmental sequence in small groups. *Psychological Bulletin*, 63(6), 384-399.

[Schein(2010)] Schein, E.H. (2010). *Organizational Culture and Leadership*. Jossey-Bass.

Resources and Partnerships

In the dynamic landscape of technological innovation, particularly in the field of immersive environments, the availability of resources and the establishment of strategic partnerships are critical to the success of any initiative. For Kai Ba and the Immersive Environments Lab, this meant not only securing financial backing but also collaborating with institutions, industry leaders, and research organizations to push the boundaries of holographic technology.

Financial Resources

The initial phase of the Immersive Environments Lab was marked by the challenge of securing adequate funding. To address this, Kai Ba employed a multi-faceted approach:

- **Grants and Government Funding:** Kai Ba sought out grants from both governmental and non-governmental organizations focused on technology and innovation. For instance, the National Science Foundation (NSF) offers grants aimed at fostering research and development in emerging technologies. The lab successfully acquired a $2 million grant aimed at advancing augmented reality applications in educational settings.

- **Venture Capital:** Recognizing the potential of immersive technology in various sectors, Kai Ba pitched the lab's vision to venture capitalists specializing in tech startups. A notable partnership was formed with TechFuture Ventures, which provided an initial investment of $5 million in exchange for equity and a seat on the advisory board.

- **Crowdfunding:** To engage the community and generate grassroots support, the lab launched a crowdfunding campaign on platforms like Kickstarter. The campaign, titled "HoloWorld: A New Dimension of Learning," raised over $500,000 within a month, showcasing public interest and support for immersive educational tools.

Academic Partnerships

Collaboration with academic institutions played a pivotal role in the lab's development. By leveraging the expertise of universities, the lab was able to access cutting-edge research and technology. Key partnerships included:

- **University of Technology:** A formal partnership with the University of Technology was established, allowing students and faculty to collaborate on research projects. This partnership led to the development of a new algorithm for real-time holographic rendering, significantly improving the user experience in virtual environments.

- **Joint Research Initiatives:** The lab participated in joint research initiatives with institutions such as the Institute for Advanced Virtual Reality. This collaboration focused on the ethical implications of immersive technologies, resulting in a comprehensive report titled "Ethics in Immersive Environments: A Framework for Responsibility," which has been widely cited in academic circles.

- **Internship Programs:** The lab also initiated internship programs for students, providing hands-on experience in holographic technology. This not only nurtured talent but also fostered innovation through fresh perspectives.

Industry Collaborations

To enhance the practical applications of its research, the Immersive Environments Lab sought collaborations with industry leaders:

- **Partnerships with Tech Giants:** Collaborations with companies like HoloTech and VirtualVision allowed the lab to access advanced hardware and software tools. These partnerships resulted in the co-development of a groundbreaking holographic display that utilized a novel light-field technology, enabling lifelike visual experiences.

- **Pilot Programs in Healthcare:** The lab partnered with healthcare providers to implement pilot programs utilizing holographic simulations for medical training. One notable example was a collaboration with City Hospital, where holographic models of human anatomy were used in training sessions, leading to a 30% increase in retention rates among medical students.

- **Corporate Sponsorships:** Corporate sponsorships also provided additional funding and resources. For example, a partnership with CreativeTech resulted in the development of a new interactive platform for educational purposes, combining holography with gamification to enhance learning outcomes.

Challenges in Resource Acquisition

Despite the successes in securing resources and partnerships, the Immersive Environments Lab faced several challenges:

- **Competition for Funding:** The competitive nature of grant applications meant that not all proposals were successful. The lab had to refine its pitch and demonstrate clear, measurable outcomes to stand out among numerous applicants.

- **Aligning Goals with Partners:** Ensuring that the goals of the lab aligned with those of its partners was crucial. Misalignment could lead to conflicts or project delays. Regular communication and collaborative goal-setting sessions were essential to maintain a unified vision.

- **Navigating Intellectual Property Issues:** Collaborations often raised questions about intellectual property rights. The lab established clear agreements with partners to delineate ownership of developed technologies and findings, ensuring that all parties benefited equitably.

Conclusion

In conclusion, the establishment of the Immersive Environments Lab under Kai Ba's leadership exemplifies the importance of resource acquisition and strategic partnerships in fostering innovation. By combining financial resources, academic expertise, and industry collaborations, the lab was able to create a robust foundation for the development of holographic technologies that would revolutionize various sectors. The lessons learned from these experiences not only contributed to the lab's success but also provided a blueprint for future innovators in the realm of immersive environments.

$$R = \frac{F + A + I}{C} \tag{19}$$

Where:

- R = Resources acquired
- F = Financial resources
- A = Academic partnerships
- I = Industry collaborations
- C = Challenges faced

This equation illustrates the balance between resources acquired and the challenges faced, emphasizing that successful innovation requires navigating complexities while leveraging available resources effectively.

Early Successes and Recognition

The journey of Kai Ba and the Immersive Environments Lab was marked by a series of early successes that not only validated their innovative approach but also garnered significant recognition within both academic and industry circles. These milestones played a crucial role in establishing the lab as a leader in the field of immersive technology.

Breakthrough Holographic Demonstrations

One of the lab's first major achievements was the development of a groundbreaking holographic demonstration that captivated audiences at the International Conference on Holography and Immersive Technology. This demonstration showcased the lab's ability to create lifelike holograms that could interact with real-world objects. The technical foundation for this demonstration was based on the principles of light field technology, which allows for the capturing and rendering of light rays from multiple angles, creating a three-dimensional visual experience.

The mathematical representation of light fields can be expressed as follows:

$$L(x,y,\theta,\phi) = \int_{-\infty}^{\infty} I(x,y,z) \cdot \delta(z - f(x,y,\theta,\phi))\, dz \qquad (20)$$

where L represents the light field, I is the intensity of light at a point (x, y, z), and δ is the Dirac delta function, which ensures that light is captured at specific angles (θ, ϕ).

This demonstration not only received accolades for its technical prowess but also sparked interest from potential industry partners, leading to collaborative projects that would further enhance the lab's capabilities.

Awards and Accolades

The recognition of the lab's work was further solidified when they received the prestigious *Innovators of Tomorrow* award from the Global Technology Forum. This award was given in recognition of their contributions to the field of immersive environments and their potential for transforming various industries. The award ceremony provided Kai Ba with a platform to articulate the vision of the lab, emphasizing the importance of ethical considerations in technology development.

In his acceptance speech, Kai Ba remarked, "Innovation should not only be about technological advancement; it must also encompass the responsibility we hold towards society and the environment." This statement resonated with many attendees, positioning the lab as a thought leader in the intersection of technology and ethics.

Media Coverage and Public Engagement

The lab's early successes did not go unnoticed by the media. Major tech publications such as *Wired*, *TechCrunch*, and *The Verge* featured articles highlighting the lab's innovative work. These articles often emphasized the unique aspects of the holographic technology being developed, including its applications in education, healthcare, and entertainment.

One notable media piece, titled *The Future is Holographic*, detailed a collaborative project between the lab and a local hospital, where holographic simulations were used for surgical training. The project demonstrated how immersive environments could enhance learning experiences and improve patient outcomes. The positive reception from both the public and industry professionals amplified the lab's visibility and attracted further investment.

Collaborative Projects and Partnerships

Building on their early successes, the Immersive Environments Lab secured partnerships with leading universities and tech companies. These collaborations allowed for the pooling of resources and expertise, accelerating the development of new technologies. For instance, a partnership with a prominent university's neuroscience department led to research on how immersive environments could aid in cognitive rehabilitation for stroke patients.

The results of this research were promising, showing that patients who engaged with holographic simulations demonstrated significant improvements in motor skills compared to traditional rehabilitation methods. This finding was later published in the *Journal of Neurorehabilitation*, further establishing the lab's reputation in the academic community.

Community Impact and Outreach Programs

Recognizing the importance of community engagement, the lab initiated outreach programs aimed at inspiring young students to explore careers in technology and innovation. These programs included workshops, school visits, and interactive demonstrations of holographic technology. By engaging with local schools, the lab not only fostered interest in STEM fields but also worked to bridge the digital divide, ensuring that underrepresented communities had access to cutting-edge technology.

The success of these outreach programs was evident in the increased enrollment of students from diverse backgrounds in technology-related courses. This initiative not only contributed to the lab's mission of innovation but also highlighted the social responsibility that accompanied their technological advancements.

Conclusion

In summary, the early successes of Kai Ba and the Immersive Environments Lab were characterized by groundbreaking demonstrations, prestigious awards, extensive media coverage, impactful collaborations, and meaningful community engagement. These accomplishments not only validated their innovative approach but also set the stage for future developments that would continue to change the landscape of immersive technology. As Kai Ba often stated, "Success is not merely a destination; it is the journey of creating a better world through innovation."

Overcoming Obstacles and Doubts

In the journey of innovation, obstacles and doubts are inevitable companions. For Kai Ba, the founder of the Immersive Environments Lab, these challenges were not merely hindrances but rather critical components of his growth as an innovator. This section delves into the specific obstacles he faced, the doubts that plagued him, and how he transformed these experiences into stepping stones for success.

The Nature of Doubt

Doubt is a multifaceted emotion, often rooted in fear of failure, inadequacy, or the unknown. For Kai, doubt manifested itself in several forms:

- **Self-Doubt:** As a young innovator, Kai often questioned his capabilities. The weight of responsibility that came with leading a team and pioneering new technologies led him to compare himself with established figures in the field.

- **Skepticism from Peers:** The ambitious vision of creating holographic worlds was met with skepticism from peers and mentors alike. Many questioned the feasibility of his ideas, often citing the technological limitations of the time.

- **Funding Challenges:** Securing funding for innovative projects is notoriously challenging. Kai faced numerous rejections from investors who were reluctant to support a venture that seemed too speculative.

Theoretical Framework: Resilience and Growth Mindset

To navigate these obstacles, Kai drew upon principles from psychological theories of resilience and the growth mindset, as proposed by psychologist Carol Dweck. Resilience refers to the ability to bounce back from setbacks, while a growth mindset is the belief that abilities and intelligence can be developed through dedication and hard work.

$$\text{Resilience} = \frac{\text{Adaptability} + \text{Perseverance}}{\text{Fear of Failure}} \qquad (21)$$

This equation illustrates that resilience is enhanced when adaptability and perseverance are prioritized over fear of failure. Kai's commitment to fostering a resilient mindset within himself and his team became a cornerstone of the Immersive Environments Lab's culture.

Strategies for Overcoming Obstacles

Kai implemented several strategies to overcome the obstacles he encountered:

1. **Building a Support Network:** Understanding the importance of collaboration, Kai surrounded himself with a diverse group of mentors, peers, and advisors. This network provided not only technical expertise but also emotional support during challenging times.

2. **Embracing Failure as a Learning Tool:** Kai adopted a philosophy of viewing failures as opportunities for growth. Each setback was analyzed for lessons learned, which contributed to the refinement of his projects and ideas.

3. **Iterative Development Process:** By adopting an agile approach to development, Kai was able to iterate on his ideas quickly. This allowed for rapid prototyping and testing, which reduced the fear of failure by fostering a culture of experimentation.

Real-World Examples

Several specific instances illustrate how Kai overcame obstacles and doubts:

- **The Initial Prototype:** The first prototype of the holographic platform faced significant technical issues. Instead of viewing this as a failure, Kai organized a hackathon with his team to address the problems collaboratively. This not only resolved the issues but also strengthened team cohesion.

- **Investor Rejections:** After facing multiple rejections from potential investors, Kai decided to pivot his pitch strategy. He focused on presenting not just the technology but also the societal impact of holographic worlds. This shift in narrative attracted the attention of socially conscious investors who shared his vision.

- **Public Criticism:** During the early presentations of his work, Kai faced public criticism regarding the ethical implications of his technology. Rather than dismissing these concerns, he engaged in open dialogues with critics, which led to the incorporation of ethical considerations into the development process, thereby enhancing the credibility of his work.

Conclusion

Overcoming obstacles and doubts is an integral part of the innovation process. For Kai Ba, these challenges were not deterrents but rather catalysts for personal and professional growth. By embracing resilience, fostering a growth mindset, and employing strategic approaches to problem-solving, Kai transformed his doubts into a powerful driving force that propelled the Immersive Environments Lab toward groundbreaking achievements. His journey serves as a testament to the idea that the path to innovation is often paved with obstacles, each offering valuable lessons that shape the future of technology.

Development of the Holographic Worlds Platform

Designing the User Interface

Designing the user interface (UI) for the Holographic Worlds platform was a pivotal undertaking that combined aesthetics, functionality, and user experience. This section delves into the principles, challenges, and innovative approaches that shaped the UI design process, ensuring that it met the needs of diverse users while enhancing the immersive experience.

Theoretical Foundations of User Interface Design

The design of any user interface is grounded in several key theories and principles. The primary goal is to create an intuitive and engaging experience that allows users to navigate and interact with holographic environments seamlessly. One of the foundational theories is Norman's Design Principles, which emphasize the importance of visibility, feedback, constraints, and affordance in UI design [?].

$$UI = f(V, F, C, A) \qquad (22)$$

Where: - UI is the user interface effectiveness, - V represents visibility, - F denotes feedback, - C signifies constraints, - A stands for affordance.

Each of these elements plays a critical role in ensuring that users can easily understand and interact with the holographic content. For instance, visibility ensures that users can see the available options, while feedback provides confirmation of their actions, enhancing their confidence in navigating the interface.

Challenges in Designing Holographic User Interfaces

Creating a UI for holographic environments presents unique challenges that differ significantly from traditional 2D interfaces. One major challenge is the spatial orientation of elements. Unlike flat screens, holographic interfaces require users to interact with 3D objects in space, which can lead to confusion if not designed intuitively.

Another challenge is ensuring accessibility for all users, including those with disabilities. This necessitates the integration of voice commands, gesture recognition, and other assistive technologies to create an inclusive environment.

Moreover, the rapid evolution of technology means that designers must continuously adapt to new tools and frameworks. The integration of artificial intelligence (AI) into the UI, for example, allows for personalized experiences but also raises concerns about user data privacy and security.

Innovative Approaches to User Interface Design

To tackle these challenges, the design team employed several innovative approaches:

- **User-Centric Design:** The design process began with extensive user research, including interviews and usability testing. This approach ensured that the UI met the actual needs and preferences of users, leading to a more engaging experience.

- **Prototyping and Iteration:** Rapid prototyping allowed the team to create and test multiple versions of the UI. By gathering feedback from users at each iteration, the team could refine the interface to enhance usability and functionality.

- **Gestural and Voice Interaction:** Recognizing the limitations of traditional input methods in a holographic environment, the UI incorporated gestural controls and voice commands. This not only improved accessibility but also provided a more immersive experience, as users could interact with holographic elements naturally.

- **Dynamic Contextual Menus:** To reduce clutter and enhance usability, the UI featured dynamic menus that appeared contextually based on user actions. This approach minimized cognitive load and allowed users to focus on the content rather than the interface.

Examples of Effective User Interface Design

An exemplary implementation of the UI design principles can be seen in the healthcare application of Holographic Worlds. In this context, medical professionals can use the holographic interface to visualize complex anatomical structures. The UI was designed to allow users to manipulate these structures with simple hand gestures, providing immediate feedback through visual cues and sound effects.

Another notable example is the educational module for immersive learning. Here, the UI utilizes augmented reality overlays to enhance traditional learning materials. Students can interact with 3D models of historical artifacts, with the UI providing contextual information and interactive quizzes that adapt to their learning pace.

Conclusion

The design of the user interface for Holographic Worlds was a complex but rewarding process that required a deep understanding of user needs, technological capabilities, and design principles. By prioritizing user experience and embracing innovative approaches, the team was able to create an interface that not only met the functional requirements but also enhanced the overall immersive experience. As the platform continues to evolve, the lessons learned from this UI design process will serve as a foundation for future innovations in the field of immersive environments.

Creating Immersive Experiences

Creating immersive experiences is at the heart of the Holographic Worlds platform developed by Kai Ba and his team. Immersion, defined as the sensation of being enveloped in a virtual environment, relies on several critical components, including sensory engagement, interactivity, and emotional resonance. This subsection will explore the theories underpinning immersive experiences, the challenges faced in their creation, and exemplary applications that illustrate the impact of these experiences on users.

Theoretical Foundations of Immersion

The concept of immersion can be traced back to the work of [?], who describes it as a psychological state resulting from the interaction between the user and the virtual environment. This interaction can be quantified using the **Presence Theory**, which posits that the more a user feels present in a virtual environment, the more immersive the experience becomes. Presence can be categorized into two dimensions: *physical presence*, which refers to the sensory realism of the environment, and *social presence*, which encompasses the user's perception of social interactions within the virtual space.

To quantify immersion, we can define the **Immersion Index** I as follows:

$$I = \frac{P_{physical} + P_{social}}{2}$$

where $P_{physical}$ and P_{social} are measures of physical and social presence, respectively. A higher Immersion Index indicates a more engaging experience, which is crucial for applications in education, healthcare, and entertainment.

Challenges in Creating Immersive Experiences

Despite the theoretical foundations, creating truly immersive experiences presents numerous challenges:

- **Technological Limitations:** Current hardware, such as head-mounted displays (HMDs) and motion sensors, can restrict the level of immersion due to latency, resolution, and field of view. For instance, the latency L in a VR system can be defined as:

$$L = \frac{D}{S}$$

  where D is the distance the user moves, and S is the speed of response from the system. High latency can break the sense of presence, leading to discomfort or disorientation.

- **User Diversity:** Users come with varying levels of experience and comfort with technology. Designing for inclusivity means addressing the needs of users with disabilities and different sensory perceptions. This requires extensive user testing and adaptability in design.

- **Content Creation:** Developing high-quality, interactive content is resource-intensive. The need for realistic graphics, engaging narratives, and interactive elements demands collaboration across disciplines, including art, programming, and psychology.

- **Ethical Considerations:** As immersive experiences can significantly impact users' emotions and behaviors, ethical considerations must be addressed. For instance, the potential for addiction or escapism raises questions about the responsibility of developers in creating engaging yet safe environments.

Examples of Immersive Experiences

The Holographic Worlds platform has successfully implemented immersive experiences across various fields, showcasing the potential of holography and virtual environments:

- **Healthcare Training:** One notable example is the use of immersive simulations for surgical training. By creating realistic scenarios where medical students can practice procedures in a risk-free environment, they develop skills without the ethical dilemmas of real-life surgeries. Research by [?] indicates that such simulations significantly improve retention and performance in real-world applications.

- **Educational Environments:** The platform has also transformed traditional classrooms into interactive learning spaces. For instance, a history lesson on ancient civilizations can be enhanced by allowing students to explore a holographic recreation of a Roman forum, fostering engagement and retention. Studies show that experiential learning increases knowledge retention rates by up to 75% compared to traditional methods [?].

- **Entertainment and Gaming:** The gaming industry has embraced immersive experiences, with titles like *Half-Life: Alyx* demonstrating the power of VR to create emotionally resonant narratives. The game's design incorporates elements of interactivity and player agency, leading to a more profound connection to the story and characters. As noted by [?], user engagement in gaming is significantly heightened in immersive environments, leading to increased enjoyment and satisfaction.

- **Architectural Visualization:** Architects utilize immersive experiences to present designs to clients in a more tangible way. By walking clients through a virtual model of a building, they can better understand spatial relationships and design choices. This approach has been shown to reduce project revisions by up to 30% [?], streamlining the design process.

Conclusion

Creating immersive experiences is a complex yet rewarding endeavor that requires a multidisciplinary approach, combining technology, psychology, and creativity. The Holographic Worlds platform exemplifies how these experiences can transform industries and enhance user engagement. By addressing the challenges of technology, user diversity, content creation, and ethical considerations, innovators like Kai Ba are paving the way for a future where immersive environments become an integral part of our daily lives. As we continue to explore the boundaries of what is possible, the potential for immersive experiences to change the way we learn, work, and interact with the world is limitless.

Integrating Artificial Intelligence

The integration of Artificial Intelligence (AI) into the Holographic Worlds platform represents a significant leap in creating immersive environments that are not only realistic but also interactive and adaptive. This section explores the theoretical foundations, challenges, and practical applications of AI within holographic environments.

Theoretical Foundations of AI in Immersive Environments

Artificial Intelligence encompasses a wide range of technologies that enable machines to mimic human cognitive functions such as learning, reasoning, and problem-solving. The primary theories that underlie AI applications in immersive environments include:

- **Machine Learning (ML):** A subset of AI that focuses on the development of algorithms that allow computers to learn from and make predictions based on data. In the context of holographic worlds, ML can be employed to analyze user interactions and adapt the environment accordingly.

- **Natural Language Processing (NLP):** This area of AI enables machines to understand and respond to human language. NLP can enhance user interaction within holographic environments by allowing users to communicate naturally with AI characters or systems.

- **Computer Vision (CV):** The ability of machines to interpret and understand visual information from the world. In holographic environments, CV can be used to track user movements and gestures, making interactions more intuitive.

The integration of these theories allows for a more dynamic and engaging user experience, where the environment responds in real-time to user actions.

Challenges in Integrating AI

While the potential of AI in holographic environments is immense, several challenges must be addressed:

- **Data Privacy and Security:** The collection of user data for AI training raises significant privacy concerns. Ensuring that data is handled securely and ethically is paramount. The equation representing data privacy can be expressed as:

$$P(D) = \frac{S(D)}{C(D)} \qquad (23)$$

where $P(D)$ represents the privacy level of data D, $S(D)$ is the security measures applied, and $C(D)$ is the complexity of the data.

- **Bias in AI Algorithms:** AI systems are susceptible to biases present in training data, which can lead to unfair or discriminatory outcomes. Addressing bias requires continuous monitoring and refinement of AI models.

- **Real-time Processing:** The need for real-time interaction in holographic environments demands high computational power. Efficient algorithms and hardware capable of processing data quickly are essential to ensure a seamless user experience.

Applications of AI in Holographic Worlds

The integration of AI into holographic environments has led to numerous innovative applications:

- **Adaptive Learning Environments:** In educational settings, AI can tailor content to individual learning styles and paces. For example, an AI tutor in a holographic classroom can assess a student's progress and modify the curriculum accordingly.

- **Virtual Companions:** AI-driven characters can provide companionship and support in immersive environments. These companions can learn from user interactions, creating personalized experiences that enhance engagement.

- **Smart Environments:** Holographic worlds can be equipped with AI systems that monitor user behavior and adjust the environment accordingly. For instance, lighting, sound, and visual elements can be altered based on user preferences and actions.

Case Study: HoloHealth

One notable example of AI integration in holographic environments is HoloHealth, a platform designed for healthcare training. HoloHealth utilizes AI to create realistic patient simulations that adapt based on the actions of medical trainees. The AI analyzes trainee decisions and provides real-time feedback, enhancing the learning experience.

The effectiveness of HoloHealth can be quantified using the following performance metric:

$$E = \frac{T_{success}}{T_{total}} \quad (24)$$

where E is the effectiveness of the training, $T_{success}$ is the time taken to successfully complete a training module, and T_{total} is the total time spent in training.

In a study conducted with medical students, HoloHealth showed a 30% increase in training efficiency compared to traditional methods, demonstrating the potential of AI-enhanced holographic platforms in professional education.

Conclusion

Integrating Artificial Intelligence into holographic environments is not merely an enhancement; it is a transformative element that redefines user interaction and experience. While challenges such as data privacy, algorithmic bias, and real-time processing must be addressed, the potential applications of AI in creating adaptive, engaging, and personalized experiences are vast. As technology continues to evolve, the synergy between AI and holographic worlds promises to unlock new dimensions of innovation and creativity.

Pushing the Boundaries of Realism

In the realm of holographic environments, realism serves as a critical benchmark for evaluating the effectiveness of immersive experiences. The quest for realism involves not only the visual fidelity of holograms but also the integration of sensory feedback, interactivity, and contextual relevance. This section delves into the theoretical underpinnings, challenges, and examples that define the pursuit of realism in holographic worlds.

Theoretical Foundations

Realism in virtual environments can be understood through the lens of several theories, including the **Media Richness Theory** and the **Presence Theory**. Media Richness Theory posits that richer media (i.e., those that convey more information) lead to better communication and understanding. In holographic environments, the richness is derived from the combination of visual, auditory, and haptic stimuli, which contribute to a sense of presence—the feeling of being "there" in the virtual space.

Presence Theory further expands this idea by defining presence as the psychological state where users feel immersed in a virtual environment. The perception of realism is a function of several factors, including:

$$\text{Perceived Realism} = f(\text{Visual Fidelity}, \text{Audio Fidelity}, \text{Interactivity}, \text{Contextual Relevance}) \tag{25}$$

Where: - Visual Fidelity refers to the quality and detail of the holographic images. - Audio Fidelity encompasses the spatial accuracy and clarity of sound. - Interactivity measures the extent to which users can engage with the environment. - Contextual Relevance assesses how well the virtual elements align with users' expectations and real-world experiences.

Challenges in Achieving Realism

Despite advancements in technology, several challenges impede the pursuit of realism in holographic worlds. These challenges include:

1. **Rendering Limitations:** High-quality rendering of holographic images requires significant computational power. The challenge lies in balancing visual fidelity with real-time performance. Techniques such as *Level of Detail* (LOD) and *Dynamic Resolution Scaling* are employed to optimize rendering without sacrificing quality.

2. **Latency Issues:** Latency, or the delay between user input and system response, can severely diminish the sense of realism. According to the *Fitts' Law*, the time it takes to reach a target is a function of the distance to the

target and the size of the target. Minimizing latency is crucial for maintaining user engagement and immersion.

$$\text{Time} \propto \frac{\text{Distance}}{\text{Target Size}} \qquad (26)$$

3. **Sensory Overload:** While rich sensory input enhances realism, excessive stimuli can lead to sensory overload, causing discomfort or disorientation. Striking a balance between immersion and usability is essential.

4. **User Variability:** Individual differences in perception, cognitive load, and sensory processing can affect how realism is experienced. Customizable settings that allow users to adjust visual and auditory parameters can help mitigate these issues.

Examples of Realism in Holographic Worlds

Several projects exemplify the successful push towards realism in holographic environments:

- **The Holodeck Project:** Inspired by science fiction, this project aims to create a fully immersive environment where users can interact with realistic holograms. Utilizing advanced motion capture and haptic feedback, users can manipulate objects in a way that feels authentic, enhancing the overall sense of presence.

- **HoloLens in Medical Training:** Microsoft's HoloLens has been employed in medical training to create realistic surgical simulations. By integrating high-fidelity visuals with real-time feedback, trainees can practice procedures in a risk-free environment, improving their skills and confidence.

- **Virtual Reality in Architecture:** Architects are using VR to visualize designs in real-time. Tools like *Enscape* allow architects to walk through their designs, experiencing spatial relationships and lighting in a way that traditional 2D models cannot provide. This immersive experience aids in making informed design decisions.

- **Gaming and Entertainment:** Games like *Half-Life: Alyx* have set new standards for realism in gaming by combining high-quality graphics, spatial audio, and interactive environments. The game's design encourages players to engage with the environment, fostering a deeper sense of immersion.

Conclusion

Pushing the boundaries of realism in holographic worlds is a multifaceted endeavor that requires a blend of technological innovation, theoretical understanding, and user-centered design. As the field evolves, the integration of advanced rendering techniques, reduced latency, and personalized experiences will continue to enhance the realism of these environments. The ongoing dialogue between creators and users will ultimately shape the future of holographic experiences, ensuring they not only reflect reality but also expand the horizons of human imagination.

Challenges in Software Development

The development of the Holographic Worlds platform is not without its challenges, particularly in the realm of software development. As Kai Ba and his team embarked on this ambitious project, they encountered various technical and conceptual obstacles that required innovative solutions and adaptive strategies. This section delves into the key challenges faced during the software development process, examining the theoretical underpinnings, practical implications, and real-world examples that illustrate these hurdles.

Complexity of Holographic Rendering

One of the primary challenges in developing holographic environments is the complexity of rendering realistic and immersive holographic visuals. Holography relies on capturing and reconstructing light fields in three dimensions, which is computationally intensive. The rendering process must account for various factors, including light propagation, surface interactions, and viewer perspective.

The rendering equation, which describes the light transport in a scene, is given by:

$$L_o(p,\omega_o) = L_e(p,\omega_o) + \int_H f_r(p,\omega_i,\omega_o) L_i(p,\omega_i) \cos(\theta_i) d\omega_i \quad (27)$$

where: - L_o is the outgoing light, - L_e is the emitted light, - f_r is the bidirectional reflectance distribution function (BRDF), - L_i is the incoming light, - θ_i is the angle of incidence, - H is the hemisphere above point p.

The challenge lies in efficiently solving this equation in real-time, as traditional methods often lead to high latency, which can detract from the immersive experience. Techniques such as ray tracing and rasterization are computationally expensive, and optimizing these methods for real-time holographic rendering remains a significant challenge.

Integration of Artificial Intelligence

The integration of artificial intelligence (AI) into the Holographic Worlds platform poses its own set of challenges. AI can enhance user experiences by providing adaptive interactions and personalized content, but developing robust AI algorithms that can operate seamlessly within a holographic environment is complex.

One major issue is the need for real-time data processing. AI models often require substantial computational resources, which can lead to delays if not managed properly. The use of techniques such as edge computing can mitigate this issue, allowing data processing to occur closer to the user, thus reducing latency. However, implementing such systems requires careful architectural planning and resource allocation.

Moreover, ensuring that AI systems operate ethically and transparently in holographic environments is crucial. This includes addressing biases in AI algorithms and ensuring that user data is handled securely. The challenge is to create a framework that allows for AI-driven interactions while maintaining user trust and safety.

User Interface Design

Creating an intuitive user interface (UI) for holographic environments is another significant challenge. Unlike traditional 2D interfaces, holographic UIs must account for spatial interactions and the three-dimensional nature of the medium. This requires a departure from conventional design principles and an understanding of how users interact with holographic content.

Designing for spatial cognition involves understanding how users perceive and interact with 3D objects. For instance, the use of gesture-based controls can enhance immersion, but designers must ensure that these gestures are natural and easily learnable. Studies indicate that users often struggle with complex gesture sets, leading to frustration and disengagement. Therefore, iterative testing and user feedback are essential in developing an effective holographic UI.

Moreover, accessibility is a critical consideration. Ensuring that holographic environments are usable by individuals with varying abilities requires thoughtful design and implementation. This includes providing alternative interaction methods and ensuring that visual elements are perceivable by all users.

Cross-Platform Compatibility

As the Holographic Worlds platform aims to reach a wide audience, ensuring cross-platform compatibility presents a significant challenge. Users may access the platform through various devices, including headsets, smartphones, and computers, each with different capabilities and limitations.

Developing software that can seamlessly operate across these platforms requires a flexible architecture and careful consideration of hardware constraints. For example, the computational power available on a high-end VR headset differs vastly from that of a mobile device. Therefore, developers must create adaptive systems that can scale their performance based on the device's capabilities.

Frameworks such as Unity and Unreal Engine have made strides in addressing cross-platform compatibility, but challenges remain in optimizing performance and ensuring consistent user experiences across devices. This requires ongoing testing and refinement to ensure that the holographic environments remain engaging and functional, regardless of the platform used.

Security and Privacy Concerns

As the Holographic Worlds platform collects and processes vast amounts of user data, security and privacy become paramount concerns. Users must feel confident that their personal information is protected, especially in immersive environments where interactions can be deeply personal and revealing.

Implementing robust security protocols is essential, including encryption, secure data storage, and user authentication mechanisms. Moreover, developers must be transparent about data usage and provide users with control over their information. This includes options for data sharing and the ability to delete personal data from the system.

The challenge lies in balancing user privacy with the need for data to enhance AI-driven experiences. Developers must navigate the complexities of data ethics and compliance with regulations such as the General Data Protection Regulation (GDPR) while still providing a rich, personalized experience.

Conclusion

In conclusion, the challenges in software development for the Holographic Worlds platform are multifaceted and require a combination of technical expertise, innovative thinking, and user-centered design. From rendering complexities and AI integration to UI design, cross-platform compatibility, and security concerns, each challenge presents opportunities for growth and innovation. As Kai Ba and his team continue to push the boundaries of what is possible in holographic environments, overcoming these obstacles will be crucial in realizing their vision of immersive, interactive worlds.

Applications in Various Fields

Holographic Worlds in Healthcare

The integration of holographic worlds in healthcare represents a groundbreaking evolution in medical practice and education. As the field of medicine increasingly embraces technology, the use of holography offers transformative potential across various dimensions, including surgical training, patient treatment, and collaborative research. This subsection delves into the theoretical foundations, practical applications, challenges, and future implications of holographic technologies in healthcare.

Theoretical Foundations

Holography, as a technique for recording and reconstructing light fields, enables the creation of three-dimensional images that can be viewed without the need for special glasses. This technology is grounded in wavefront reconstruction principles, where the interference pattern of light waves is captured on a medium. Mathematically, the holographic process can be described by the equation:

$$H(x,y) = \int\int I(x',y')e^{j\phi(x',y')}dx'dy' \qquad (28)$$

where $H(x,y)$ is the hologram, $I(x',y')$ is the intensity of the light field, and $\phi(x',y')$ is the phase information. The ability to manipulate these holograms in real-time allows healthcare professionals to visualize complex anatomical structures and physiological processes in a more intuitive manner.

Applications in Surgical Training

One of the most promising applications of holographic worlds in healthcare is in surgical training. Traditional methods often rely on two-dimensional images or physical models, which can limit the depth of understanding. Holographic simulations provide a more immersive experience, allowing trainees to interact with lifelike representations of human anatomy.

For example, the use of holographic displays in surgical simulations can enhance the learning experience by allowing medical students to visualize and practice procedures in a risk-free environment. A study conducted at the University of California demonstrated that surgical residents trained with holographic visualization techniques performed significantly better in laparoscopic procedures compared to those trained with conventional methods [1].

Enhancing Patient Treatment

Holographic worlds also have the potential to revolutionize patient treatment protocols. By creating personalized holographic representations of a patient's anatomy, healthcare providers can tailor treatment plans more effectively. This is particularly beneficial in fields such as oncology, where understanding the precise location and size of tumors is critical for successful intervention.

In a groundbreaking case, a team of surgeons at Johns Hopkins University utilized holographic technology to visualize a patient's complex vascular structure prior to a high-risk surgery. This preparation allowed them to devise a more effective surgical approach, ultimately leading to improved patient outcomes [2].

Collaborative Research and Remote Consultations

Holographic worlds facilitate collaboration among medical professionals, enabling remote consultations and joint surgeries. By sharing holographic models of patients, specialists can provide insights and recommendations from different geographic locations. This capability is particularly advantageous in emergency situations where time is of the essence.

For instance, during the COVID-19 pandemic, healthcare providers employed holographic technology to conduct remote consultations, allowing specialists to guide on-site medical teams through complex procedures without being physically present. This not only ensured timely interventions but also minimized the risk of virus transmission [3].

Challenges and Ethical Considerations

Despite the promising applications of holographic worlds in healthcare, several challenges must be addressed. One major concern is the accuracy and reliability of holographic representations. Inaccurate models could lead to misdiagnosis or inappropriate treatment plans. Therefore, it is essential to establish rigorous validation protocols for holographic systems.

Additionally, ethical considerations surrounding patient data privacy and consent are paramount. The use of holographic technology necessitates the handling of sensitive patient information, which must be protected to maintain trust and comply with regulations such as the Health Insurance Portability and Accountability Act (HIPAA).

Future Implications

Looking ahead, the integration of holographic worlds in healthcare is poised to expand further. As technology advances, we can expect more sophisticated holographic systems that incorporate artificial intelligence and machine learning to enhance diagnostic accuracy and treatment efficacy.

Moreover, the potential for augmented reality (AR) and virtual reality (VR) integration with holography could lead to even more immersive and interactive healthcare experiences. For instance, combining holographic visualizations with real-time data from wearable health devices could provide clinicians with comprehensive insights into a patient's condition.

In conclusion, holographic worlds in healthcare represent a revolutionary shift in medical practice, offering innovative solutions for surgical training, patient treatment, and collaborative research. While challenges remain, the potential benefits of this technology are immense, paving the way for a future where holography plays a central role in improving healthcare outcomes.

Bibliography

[1] University of California. (2023). *Impact of Holographic Training on Surgical Performance*. Journal of Surgical Education.

[2] Johns Hopkins University. (2023). *Innovative Use of Holography in Complex Vascular Surgery*. Journal of Medical Innovation.

[3] Healthcare Innovations. (2023). *Remote Consultations During COVID-19: The Role of Holographic Technology*. International Journal of Telemedicine.

Revolutionizing Education and Training

The advent of holographic worlds has ushered in a new era in education and training, transforming traditional pedagogical methods and creating immersive learning environments. By leveraging advanced technologies such as holography, augmented reality (AR), and virtual reality (VR), educators can now offer experiences that engage students in ways previously thought impossible. This section explores the theoretical foundations, practical applications, and challenges associated with using holographic technologies in educational settings.

Theoretical Foundations

The integration of holographic technologies in education aligns with several key educational theories, including constructivism and experiential learning.

Constructivism posits that learners construct knowledge through experiences and interactions with their environment. Holographic environments provide a dynamic space where learners can manipulate objects and engage in problem-solving tasks, fostering deeper understanding. According to Piaget's theory of cognitive development, active engagement in learning leads to better retention and comprehension.

Experiential Learning Theory (Kolb, 1984) emphasizes the importance of hands-on experience in the learning process. The four stages of experiential learning—concrete experience, reflective observation, abstract conceptualization, and active experimentation—are inherently supported by holographic simulations, allowing learners to engage in realistic scenarios that promote critical thinking and application of knowledge.

Practical Applications

Holographic worlds have been successfully implemented across various educational domains, demonstrating their versatility and effectiveness in enhancing learning outcomes.

Medical Training is one of the most prominent examples of holographic technology's impact on education. Medical students can practice surgical procedures in a risk-free environment, interacting with 3D holographic models of human anatomy. For instance, the use of holographic simulations in surgical training allows students to visualize complex structures and practice techniques before performing on real patients, significantly improving their skills and confidence.

STEM Education has also benefited from holographic learning environments. Programs such as HoloLab, which allow students to conduct chemistry experiments in a virtual lab, enable learners to manipulate molecules and observe reactions in real-time. This not only enhances understanding of abstract concepts but also fosters a sense of inquiry and experimentation.

Language Learning is another area where holographic worlds can revolutionize training. Immersive environments can simulate real-life scenarios, such as ordering food in a restaurant or navigating a foreign city. By interacting with holographic characters, learners can practice conversational skills and cultural nuances in a safe and engaging manner.

Challenges and Considerations

Despite the promising potential of holographic education, several challenges must be addressed to ensure its effective implementation.

Access and Equity is a significant concern, as not all students have equal access to advanced technologies. Schools in underfunded areas may struggle to acquire the necessary hardware and software, potentially exacerbating existing educational disparities. Policymakers must prioritize equitable access to technology to ensure all students can benefit from these innovations.

Teacher Training is another critical factor. Educators must be adequately trained to utilize holographic technologies effectively. This includes not only technical skills but also pedagogical strategies to integrate these tools into their teaching practices. Professional development programs should be established to support teachers in this transition.

Cognitive Overload is a potential risk when using immersive environments. While engaging, excessive sensory input can overwhelm learners, hindering their ability to focus and retain information. Designers of holographic educational experiences must strike a balance between immersion and cognitive load, ensuring that learners remain engaged without becoming overwhelmed.

Conclusion

The integration of holographic worlds into education and training represents a paradigm shift in how knowledge is imparted and acquired. By providing immersive, interactive experiences that align with established educational theories, holographic technologies have the potential to enhance learning outcomes across various domains. However, addressing challenges related to access, teacher training, and cognitive overload is essential for realizing the full benefits of this revolutionary approach. As we continue to explore the possibilities of holographic education, it is crucial to prioritize inclusivity and support for educators to create a future where immersive learning experiences are accessible to all.

$$\text{Learning Outcome} = f(\text{Engagement, Experience, Reflection}) \quad (29)$$

In this equation, the learning outcome is a function of engagement, experience, and reflection, emphasizing the interconnectedness of these elements in the context of holographic education.

Transforming Entertainment and Gaming

The advent of holographic technology has ushered in a new era in entertainment and gaming, redefining how individuals experience stories, interact with characters, and engage in gameplay. This transformation is not merely a technological upgrade but a paradigm shift that encompasses immersive storytelling, social interaction, and the blurring of lines between the virtual and the real.

Theoretical Framework

At the core of this transformation lies the concept of immersion, which can be defined as the degree to which a user feels absorbed in a virtual environment. According to the *Immersive Experience Theory*, immersion comprises three dimensions: *sensory immersion, cognitive immersion,* and *emotional immersion* [Slater & Wilbur, 2009].

$$\text{Immersion} = f(\text{Sensory Immersion, Cognitive Immersion, Emotional Immersion}) \tag{30}$$

Where: - Sensory immersion refers to the extent to which the environment stimulates the senses. - Cognitive immersion describes the mental engagement and presence within the narrative. - Emotional immersion pertains to the feelings and emotional responses elicited by the experience.

Innovative Applications in Gaming

Holographic technology has enabled a variety of innovative applications in gaming, allowing players to interact with characters and environments in unprecedented ways. For instance, the game *HoloQuest* utilizes holographic displays to project characters that players can physically interact with, creating a tactile experience that traditional gaming cannot replicate. Players can engage in quests where they must solve puzzles with holographic characters that respond to their movements and voice commands, effectively merging physical and digital realms.

Challenges in Implementation

Despite the promise of holographic gaming, several challenges remain. One significant issue is the *technical limitations* of current holographic displays, which often struggle to maintain high resolution and depth perception, particularly in outdoor settings or large environments. Furthermore, the *cost* of developing and deploying holographic systems can be prohibitive, limiting access to these experiences for the average consumer.

Moreover, the *social implications* of immersive gaming experiences must be considered. As players increasingly engage with virtual characters and worlds, questions arise about the impact on real-life social interactions. A study by Przybylski and Weinstein (2019) suggests that while immersive gaming can foster social connections, excessive engagement may lead to social isolation [?].

Case Studies

Several case studies exemplify the transformative potential of holographic technology in entertainment and gaming:

1. **Star Wars: Hologram Adventures**: This interactive experience allows fans to engage with holographic versions of their favorite characters, providing a unique narrative that adapts based on user choices. The experience combines storytelling with real-time interaction, creating a personalized adventure.

2. **HoloLens in Gaming**: Microsoft's HoloLens has been utilized in games like *Minecraft*, where players can build and manipulate their worlds in real-time using hand gestures and voice commands. This integration of augmented reality with traditional gameplay mechanics has redefined player interaction.

3. **Holographic Esports**: The rise of holographic esports tournaments has transformed competitive gaming. Spectators can watch matches unfold in 3D, gaining insights into player strategies through holographic overlays that provide real-time statistics and analyses.

Future Directions

Looking ahead, the future of holographic entertainment and gaming is promising. The integration of artificial intelligence (AI) is expected to enhance the interactivity of holographic characters, allowing them to adapt and respond to player behaviors in real-time. This could lead to more personalized gaming experiences, where narratives evolve based on individual choices.

Moreover, advancements in holographic display technology will likely address current limitations, enabling more widespread adoption in homes and public spaces. As the technology becomes more accessible, the potential for community-driven experiences—where players collaborate in shared holographic environments—will grow, fostering new forms of social interaction and collective storytelling.

Conclusion

In conclusion, holographic technology is not just transforming entertainment and gaming; it is redefining the very nature of interaction and immersion. As the barriers between the virtual and the real continue to blur, the potential for innovative storytelling and engagement will expand, promising a future where entertainment is more interactive, immersive, and socially connected than ever before.

Impact on Architecture and Design

The advent of holographic worlds has revolutionized the fields of architecture and design, offering unprecedented opportunities for visualization, collaboration, and innovation. This section explores the multifaceted impact of holographic technology on architectural practices, examining both theoretical frameworks and practical applications.

Enhanced Visualization Techniques

One of the most significant contributions of holographic technology to architecture is the ability to create immersive visualizations that transcend traditional 2D representations. Architects can now present their designs in a three-dimensional space, allowing clients and stakeholders to experience the project before it is built. This shift from flat renderings to holographic models enables a more intuitive understanding of scale, proportion, and spatial relationships.

$$V = L \times W \times H \qquad (31)$$

Where V is the volume of the space, L is the length, W is the width, and H is the height. Holographic models can be manipulated in real-time, allowing users to alter dimensions and explore various design iterations dynamically.

Collaborative Design Processes

Holographic environments facilitate collaborative design processes by enabling multiple stakeholders to interact with the digital model simultaneously. This is particularly beneficial in large-scale projects where input from various disciplines—such as engineering, landscape architecture, and urban planning—is crucial. Using holographic interfaces, team members can visualize changes in real-time, fostering a more integrated approach to design.

For instance, the architectural firm *Foster + Partners* has utilized holographic technology in the design of the *Apple Park* in Cupertino, California. By employing mixed-reality tools, the team was able to collaborate effectively across continents, sharing insights and making adjustments instantly.

Sustainability and Resource Management

The integration of holographic technology in architecture also promotes sustainable design practices. By simulating environmental conditions and assessing the impact of design choices, architects can make informed decisions that minimize resource consumption. Holographic models can simulate sunlight patterns, wind flow, and energy usage, allowing architects to optimize building orientation and materials for enhanced energy efficiency.

$$E = \frac{P}{t} \tag{32}$$

Where E is energy consumption, P is power, and t is time. By visualizing energy flows within a holographic model, architects can identify areas for improvement and implement strategies that lead to reduced carbon footprints.

Problem-Solving and Innovation

Holographic worlds encourage innovative problem-solving by allowing architects to experiment with unconventional designs and materials. For example, the concept of biomimicry—design inspired by natural systems—can be explored in depth through holographic simulations. Architects can visualize how structures mimic natural forms, leading to designs that are both aesthetically pleasing and functionally efficient.

A notable example is the *Eden Project* in Cornwall, UK, which employs geodesic domes inspired by natural structures. Holographic technology allowed the design team to simulate various environmental conditions and assess the performance of their biomimetic designs before construction began.

Challenges and Ethical Considerations

Despite the advantages, the use of holographic technology in architecture presents several challenges. The reliance on digital tools raises questions about accessibility and equity in design processes. Not all stakeholders may have equal access to the technology, potentially leading to disparities in participation and representation.

Moreover, as architects increasingly rely on virtual models, there is a risk of detachment from the physical realities of construction. The complexity of translating holographic designs into tangible structures requires careful consideration of materiality, context, and human experience.

Conclusion

In conclusion, the impact of holographic worlds on architecture and design is profound, offering new avenues for visualization, collaboration, and sustainability. While challenges remain, the potential for innovation and improved design practices is immense. As technology continues to evolve, the architectural landscape will likely be transformed, enabling designers to create spaces that are not only functional but also deeply resonant with the human experience.

Holographic Worlds in Sports

The integration of holographic technology into the realm of sports has opened up new frontiers for both athletes and fans alike. Holographic worlds are redefining how sports are experienced, trained for, and consumed, leading to significant changes in performance analysis, fan engagement, and even the very nature of competition itself.

Enhancing Training and Performance

One of the most significant applications of holographic technology in sports is in the area of training and performance enhancement. Holographic environments allow athletes to engage in simulated scenarios that replicate real-world competition without the physical wear and tear associated with traditional training methods.

For instance, consider the following equation that models the impact of holographic training on an athlete's performance improvement:

$$P_{new} = P_{old} + \Delta P \qquad (33)$$

Where: - P_{new} is the new performance level, - P_{old} is the old performance level, and - ΔP represents the performance gain achieved through holographic training.

The use of holograms enables athletes to visualize their movements and techniques in real-time, receiving instant feedback that can be crucial for refining their skills. For example, a basketball player can practice free throws while receiving holographic overlays that display optimal shooting angles and trajectories, allowing them to adjust their form dynamically.

Injury Rehabilitation

Holographic worlds also play a vital role in injury rehabilitation. Athletes recovering from injuries can utilize holographic simulations to engage in low-impact exercises tailored to their specific recovery needs. This technology allows them to maintain their fitness levels while minimizing the risk of re-injury.

A study conducted by the Sports Science Institute found that athletes who participated in holographic rehabilitation programs showed a 30% faster recovery rate compared to those undergoing traditional physical therapy. The immersive nature of holography keeps athletes engaged and motivated during their recovery process, which is critical for mental well-being.

Fan Engagement and Experience

Holographic technology is not limited to training and performance; it has also transformed the way fans engage with their favorite sports. Holographic displays at stadiums and events provide fans with immersive experiences that enhance their enjoyment of the game.

For example, during halftime shows, holographic performances can bring to life stunning visuals that interact with the players on the field. Fans can also utilize augmented reality (AR) applications on their devices to view holographic replays, player statistics, and even interactive content that enhances their understanding of the game.

Virtual Competitions

The rise of holographic technology has also given birth to new forms of competition. Virtual sports leagues, where athletes compete in holographic environments, are becoming increasingly popular. These leagues allow for a diverse range of sports to be played in a fully immersive setting, attracting a global audience.

An example of this is the HoloLeague, a virtual sports league that features holographic versions of traditional sports such as soccer, basketball, and even extreme sports. Athletes can compete from anywhere in the world, and the holographic representation allows for unprecedented levels of interaction and competition.

Ethical Considerations and Challenges

Despite the numerous benefits of holographic worlds in sports, there are also ethical considerations and challenges that must be addressed. Issues such as data privacy, the digital divide, and the potential for addiction to virtual competitions are becoming increasingly relevant.

For example, athletes' performance data collected during holographic training sessions must be handled with care to prevent misuse. Additionally, access to advanced holographic training facilities may be limited to well-funded teams, creating disparities in opportunities for athletes from different backgrounds.

Conclusion

In conclusion, the integration of holographic worlds into sports is revolutionizing the industry in ways that were previously unimaginable. From enhancing training and rehabilitation to transforming fan engagement and creating new forms of competition, the possibilities are vast. However, it is essential to navigate the ethical landscape carefully to ensure that the benefits of this technology are accessible to all and that the integrity of sports is maintained.

As we look to the future, it is clear that holographic technology will continue to play a pivotal role in shaping the sports industry, pushing the boundaries of what is possible and redefining the very essence of athletic competition.

Facing Challenges and Changing the World

Holographic Worlds Beyond Earth

Exploring Space through Virtual Reality

The advent of Virtual Reality (VR) technology has revolutionized the way we explore and understand space. By creating immersive environments that simulate the vastness of the universe, VR allows users to experience celestial phenomena, navigate spacecraft, and participate in missions that would otherwise be impossible. This subsection delves into the theoretical underpinnings of VR in space exploration, the challenges faced, and notable examples that illustrate its impact.

Theoretical Framework

At its core, VR operates on principles of perception and immersion. The primary theory underpinning VR is the concept of *presence*, which refers to the sensation of being physically present in a virtual environment. This sensation is achieved through a combination of sensory inputs—visual, auditory, and haptic—that engage the user and create a convincing illusion of reality.

Mathematically, the effectiveness of VR can be described through the *Sense of Presence Equation*:

$$P = f(V, A, H, C) \qquad (34)$$

where P represents the sense of presence, V is the visual fidelity, A is the auditory realism, H is the haptic feedback, and C is the contextual relevance of the experience.

High levels of each component contribute to a more profound sense of immersion, allowing users to engage with complex space environments effectively.

Challenges in VR Space Exploration

Despite its potential, exploring space through VR is fraught with challenges:

- **Technical Limitations:** High-fidelity graphics and real-time rendering require significant computational power. Current VR systems may struggle to replicate the intricacies of space phenomena, such as the subtle variations in light and texture found on celestial bodies.

- **Data Integration:** Space missions generate vast amounts of data. Integrating this data into a VR environment in a meaningful way poses significant challenges. For instance, how can real-time data from Mars rovers be effectively visualized for users on Earth?

- **User Experience:** Designing intuitive interfaces that cater to both novice users and experienced astronauts is essential. The balance between complexity and usability can impact the overall effectiveness of the VR experience.

- **Physical Discomfort:** Prolonged use of VR can lead to discomfort or motion sickness due to discrepancies between visual and physical movement. Addressing these issues is critical to ensure that users can engage with VR environments comfortably.

Notable Examples

Several pioneering projects illustrate the transformative potential of VR in space exploration:

- **NASA's Mars Exploration Program:** NASA has integrated VR into its Mars exploration initiatives. The *Mars 2030* project allows users to experience the Martian surface as if they were physically present, using real data from the Curiosity rover. Users can navigate the terrain, collect samples, and understand the challenges of living on Mars.

- **SpaceVR:** This startup aims to provide immersive experiences of space travel through VR. By using footage from the ISS (International Space Station), SpaceVR enables users to experience a spacewalk or observe Earth from orbit. Their platform emphasizes education, allowing users to learn about space science while engaging in a virtual environment.

- **Virtual Reality Spacewalks:** Developed by the European Space Agency (ESA), this VR application simulates the experience of an astronaut performing a spacewalk. Users can interact with tools and navigate the exterior of the ISS, gaining insight into the complexities of astronaut tasks in microgravity.

- **The Universe Sandbox:** This interactive simulation software allows users to manipulate celestial bodies and observe the resulting gravitational interactions. It serves as both an educational tool and a platform for experimentation, showcasing the principles of astrophysics in an engaging manner.

Conclusion

Exploring space through virtual reality not only enhances our understanding of the universe but also democratizes access to space experiences. By overcoming technical challenges and integrating real-time data, VR has the potential to transform how we engage with space exploration. As technology advances, the immersive experiences offered by VR will continue to evolve, opening new frontiers for education, research, and public engagement in the cosmos.

The future of space exploration is not just about the physical journey beyond our planet; it is equally about the virtual journeys that bring the wonders of the universe closer to home.

Remote Collaboration in Space Missions

The advent of holographic technology has revolutionized the way we approach remote collaboration in space missions. As humanity reaches further into the cosmos, the need for effective communication and teamwork among astronauts, scientists, and engineers becomes paramount. This subsection explores the theoretical frameworks, challenges, and practical examples of remote collaboration facilitated by holographic worlds.

Theoretical Frameworks

Remote collaboration in space missions hinges on several theoretical models, including the **Media Richness Theory** and the **Social Presence Theory**.

Media Richness Theory Media Richness Theory posits that different communication media vary in their ability to convey information effectively. Holographic interfaces are considered high-richness media, capable of transmitting visual, auditory, and spatial information simultaneously. This richness enhances understanding, reduces ambiguity, and fosters a sense of presence among team members, which is critical in high-stakes environments like space missions.

Social Presence Theory Social Presence Theory emphasizes the importance of feeling 'present' with others during communication. Holographic environments can simulate face-to-face interactions, allowing team members to perceive non-verbal cues such as gestures and facial expressions. This enhances trust and rapport, essential components for effective collaboration in isolated and high-pressure settings like space.

Challenges in Remote Collaboration

Despite the potential benefits, several challenges hinder effective remote collaboration in space missions:

Latency and Bandwidth Limitations One of the primary challenges in remote collaboration is the latency inherent in space communication. For instance, communication between Earth and Mars can experience delays of up to 20 minutes one way. This latency complicates real-time interactions and requires teams to develop strategies for asynchronous communication.

Technical Malfunctions Technical issues, such as software bugs or hardware failures, can disrupt collaboration. For example, during the Mars Exploration Rover missions, communication systems occasionally faced disruptions due to solar interference. Such incidents highlight the need for robust backup systems and contingency plans.

Cultural and Linguistic Differences As missions become more international, team members may come from diverse cultural and linguistic backgrounds. Misunderstandings arising from these differences can lead to conflicts or errors in mission execution. Holographic environments must incorporate features that facilitate cross-cultural communication, such as real-time translation and cultural sensitivity training.

Practical Examples

Several space missions have successfully implemented holographic technologies to enhance remote collaboration:

NASA's Artemis Program   The Artemis program aims to return humans to the Moon and establish a sustainable presence there. NASA has been exploring the use of holographic interfaces for training astronauts and coordinating with ground control. Holographic simulations allow astronauts to practice complex procedures in a lifelike environment, enhancing their preparedness for actual missions.

International Space Station (ISS) Collaborations   The ISS serves as a platform for international collaboration in space research. Holographic technology has been tested for remote operations, enabling scientists on Earth to assist astronauts in real-time experiments. For instance, when conducting biological experiments, scientists can guide astronauts through intricate procedures using holographic overlays that display step-by-step instructions.

Mars Mission Simulations   During training for Mars missions, teams have utilized holographic environments to simulate the Martian landscape and conditions. These simulations enable mission planners to rehearse various scenarios, from habitat construction to emergency responses, fostering teamwork and problem-solving skills in a risk-free setting.

Future Directions

Looking ahead, the integration of advanced holographic technologies in remote collaboration for space missions presents exciting possibilities:

Enhanced AI Integration   The incorporation of artificial intelligence (AI) within holographic platforms can facilitate real-time decision-making support. AI can analyze data from ongoing experiments and provide recommendations, allowing astronauts to focus on execution rather than analysis.

Interplanetary Collaboration Frameworks   As humanity expands its presence beyond Earth, establishing frameworks for interplanetary collaboration will become essential. Future missions may involve multiple teams working simultaneously on different celestial bodies. Holographic technologies will play a critical role in ensuring seamless communication and collaboration across vast distances.

Ethical Considerations As we develop these technologies, ethical considerations must guide their implementation. Ensuring equitable access to holographic tools and addressing issues related to data privacy and security will be crucial in fostering trust among international partners.

In conclusion, remote collaboration in space missions is poised for transformation through holographic technologies. By addressing existing challenges and leveraging theoretical frameworks, we can enhance teamwork, improve mission outcomes, and pave the way for humanity's future in space exploration.

Virtual Colonies on Mars

The concept of establishing virtual colonies on Mars represents a fascinating intersection of technology, sociology, and ethics. As humanity sets its sights on the red planet, the integration of holographic worlds into the planning and execution of Martian settlements could drastically alter our approach to space colonization.

Theoretical Framework

The theoretical underpinnings of virtual colonies on Mars can be explored through several lenses, including systems theory, simulation theory, and socio-technical systems. Systems theory posits that any complex system, such as a Martian colony, must be understood as a whole rather than through its individual components. This holistic approach is essential when considering the myriad factors that contribute to a successful colony, including environmental conditions, resource management, and human psychology.

Simulation theory, particularly as articulated by philosopher Nick Bostrom, suggests that advanced civilizations may create simulations indistinguishable from reality. If we apply this theory to virtual colonies, we can envision a scenario where Earth-based researchers simulate Martian environments to prepare for real-world challenges. This simulation could involve the use of holographic technology to create immersive experiences for astronauts and scientists, allowing them to interact with virtual environments that mimic the Martian landscape.

Problems and Challenges

Despite the promising potential of virtual colonies, several challenges must be addressed:

3.2.1 Environmental Simulation One of the primary challenges in creating virtual colonies on Mars is accurately simulating the Martian environment. Mars is characterized by its thin atmosphere, extreme temperatures, and dust storms. The simulation must account for these factors, requiring sophisticated algorithms and extensive data collection from Mars missions. The equation governing the atmospheric pressure on Mars, for instance, can be expressed as:

$$P = \frac{nRT}{V} \qquad (35)$$

where P is the pressure, n is the number of moles of gas, R is the ideal gas constant, T is the temperature in Kelvin, and V is the volume. Accurate modeling of these variables is crucial for creating realistic virtual environments.

3.2.2 Human Factors Another significant challenge involves human factors, particularly psychological well-being. Extended stays in isolated and confined environments like those on Mars can lead to various psychological issues, including depression and anxiety. Virtual colonies could help mitigate these effects by offering immersive experiences that allow colonists to engage with Earth-like environments, thus reducing feelings of isolation. However, researchers must carefully design these experiences to avoid creating a dependency on virtual interactions, which could detract from the colonists' ability to cope with their actual environment.

3.2.3 Technological Limitations The technological limitations of current holographic systems also pose a challenge. To create fully immersive environments, high-resolution displays, advanced haptic feedback systems, and real-time processing capabilities are necessary. The integration of artificial intelligence (AI) into these systems can enhance the realism of virtual interactions. For example, AI can simulate the behavior of Martian wildlife or the effects of weather patterns, adding depth to the virtual experience.

Examples of Virtual Colonies

Several initiatives and projects exemplify the potential of virtual colonies on Mars:

3.3.1 NASA's HI-SEAS

NASA's HI-SEAS (Hawaii Space Exploration Analog and Simulation) project has provided valuable insights into the psychological and social dynamics of living in a confined environment. Participants live in a simulated Martian habitat for extended periods, allowing researchers to study group behavior and decision-making processes. The data collected from HI-SEAS can inform the development of virtual colonies, creating realistic scenarios for future Martian settlers.

3.3.2 Virtual Reality Simulations

Various organizations, including SpaceX and the Mars Society, have begun developing virtual reality simulations of Martian environments. These simulations allow users to experience the Martian landscape, practice habitat construction, and engage in scientific research, all from the comfort of Earth. For instance, the Mars Society's Mars Virtual Reality project provides a platform for users to explore potential colony sites and experiment with different settlement designs.

3.3.3 Educational Initiatives

Educational institutions are also leveraging virtual colonies to inspire the next generation of space explorers. Programs that incorporate holographic simulations of Mars into their curricula can engage students in STEM (science, technology, engineering, and mathematics) fields, fostering interest in space exploration. By allowing students to virtually inhabit a Martian colony, educators can create a compelling narrative that highlights the challenges and opportunities of interplanetary living.

Conclusion

In conclusion, the establishment of virtual colonies on Mars presents an innovative approach to addressing the challenges of space colonization. By leveraging holographic technology, researchers and educators can create immersive environments that prepare humanity for life on the red planet. However, careful consideration of environmental, psychological, and technological factors is essential to ensure the success of these virtual endeavors. As we continue to explore the possibilities of holographic worlds, the vision of thriving colonies on Mars may one day become a reality, paving the way for humanity's next great adventure.

Human-Machine Integration in Space

The integration of human capabilities with machine intelligence in space exploration represents a significant frontier in both technology and human evolution. This subsection delves into the various dimensions of human-machine integration, emphasizing its theoretical foundations, practical challenges, and real-world applications.

Theoretical Foundations

Human-machine integration is grounded in several theoretical frameworks, including Cybernetics, Human Factors Engineering, and Systems Theory.

Cybernetics focuses on the communication and control mechanisms in complex systems. Norbert Wiener, the founder of Cybernetics, described systems that can self-regulate and adapt through feedback loops. In the context of space exploration, this means creating machines that can not only perform tasks but also learn from human actions and environmental changes.

Human Factors Engineering examines how humans interact with machines, aiming to optimize performance and safety. This discipline is particularly relevant in space missions where the stakes are high, and the environment is unforgiving.

Systems Theory provides a holistic view of the interactions between humans and machines, emphasizing the importance of context and the interdependence of components within a system.

The integration of these theories leads to the development of systems where humans and machines collaborate seamlessly, enhancing efficiency and decision-making capabilities.

Challenges in Human-Machine Integration

Despite the theoretical advancements, several challenges impede effective human-machine integration in space:

Cognitive Overload is a significant concern. Astronauts are often required to process vast amounts of information quickly. For instance, during the Apollo missions, astronauts faced numerous simultaneous data inputs from navigation systems, life support, and mission parameters. This cognitive load can lead to errors, particularly in high-stress environments.

Trust and Reliance on machines is another critical issue. Astronauts must develop trust in automated systems, such as autonomous spacecraft or robotic assistants. A study conducted by Lee and See (2004) highlights that while humans are generally inclined to trust machines, this trust can wane in unpredictable situations, potentially jeopardizing mission success.

Physical and Psychological Effects of long-duration spaceflight can also impact human-machine integration. The effects of microgravity, radiation, and isolation can alter cognitive functions and emotional states, complicating interactions with machines. For example, astronauts aboard the International Space Station (ISS) have reported increased stress levels, which can hinder their ability to operate complex systems effectively.

Examples of Human-Machine Integration in Space

Real-world applications of human-machine integration in space highlight both the potential and challenges of this collaboration:

Robotic Assistants like the Canadian Space Agency's Dextre are designed to assist astronauts in performing maintenance tasks on the ISS. Dextre can autonomously execute tasks such as replacing components and conducting inspections, reducing the need for astronauts to perform extravehicular activities (EVAs) under potentially dangerous conditions.

Autonomous Navigation Systems are being developed for future Mars missions. These systems utilize advanced algorithms to navigate spacecraft without human intervention, allowing for real-time adjustments based on environmental data. For instance, the Mars 2020 Perseverance rover employs autonomous navigation to traverse the Martian landscape, enabling it to avoid obstacles and select optimal paths for exploration.

Virtual Reality (VR) Training is increasingly being used to prepare astronauts for the challenges of space missions. By simulating the space environment, VR allows astronauts to practice interactions with machines in a controlled setting, enhancing their readiness for real-world scenarios. NASA's use of VR for training astronauts in robotic operations is a prime example of this integration.

Mathematical Modeling of Human-Machine Interaction

Mathematical models can help in understanding and improving human-machine integration. One such model is the *Human-Machine Interaction Model* (HMIM), which can be expressed as:

$$HMI = f(H, M, C) \qquad (36)$$

where:

- H represents human capabilities (cognitive, physical, emotional),
- M denotes machine capabilities (autonomy, responsiveness, reliability),
- C is the contextual factors (environmental conditions, mission complexity).

This model can be used to analyze how changes in one component affect the overall interaction, guiding the design of more effective human-machine systems.

Future Directions

Looking ahead, the integration of human and machine capabilities in space exploration will continue to evolve. Emerging technologies such as artificial intelligence (AI), machine learning, and advanced robotics will play pivotal roles in enhancing this integration.

For instance, AI algorithms could enable machines to predict human needs and adapt their functionalities accordingly, fostering a more intuitive collaboration. Moreover, as space missions extend beyond low Earth orbit, the reliance on autonomous systems will become increasingly crucial, necessitating ongoing research into effective human-machine integration strategies.

In conclusion, human-machine integration in space is a multifaceted challenge that combines theoretical insights with practical applications. By addressing the cognitive, emotional, and contextual factors that influence this integration, future missions can harness the full potential of both human ingenuity and machine intelligence, paving the way for unprecedented achievements in space exploration.

Impact on Astronomy and Space Exploration

The advent of holographic technology has significantly transformed the landscape of astronomy and space exploration. By creating immersive environments that simulate cosmic phenomena, holography enables researchers and enthusiasts to visualize and interact with the universe in unprecedented ways. This section explores the theoretical foundations, practical applications, and challenges associated with the integration of holographic worlds into the field of astronomy.

Theoretical Foundations

At the core of holographic technology lies the principle of interference and diffraction of light. Holography captures the light field of an object, creating a three-dimensional representation that can be viewed from different angles. This principle can be applied to astronomical data, allowing scientists to visualize celestial bodies and phenomena in a more intuitive manner. The holographic representation of astronomical data can be expressed mathematically as:

$$H(x,y) = \int\int I(x',y') \cdot \exp\left(-\frac{(x-x')^2 + (y-y')^2}{2\sigma^2}\right) dx'dy' \quad (37)$$

where $H(x,y)$ is the holographic image, $I(x',y')$ represents the intensity of light from the celestial object, and σ is a parameter that controls the spread of the holographic reconstruction.

Applications in Astronomy

Holographic technologies can be applied in several key areas of astronomy:

- **Data Visualization:** Holography allows astronomers to visualize complex datasets, such as those generated by telescopes and satellites. By transforming multi-dimensional data into a holographic format, researchers can explore the spatial relationships between celestial objects, leading to new insights into their formation and evolution.

- **Public Engagement:** Holographic displays can enhance public understanding of astronomy. Planetariums and science centers have begun incorporating holographic technologies to create immersive experiences that engage visitors, allowing them to explore the cosmos interactively. For instance, the use of holographic projections of constellations enables audiences to visualize star patterns in a compelling manner.

- **Remote Collaboration:** Holographic environments facilitate real-time collaboration among astronomers across the globe. Researchers can share holographic models of celestial phenomena, conduct joint analyses, and discuss findings in a shared virtual space, effectively breaking down geographical barriers.

- **Simulating Space Missions:** Holography can be employed to simulate space missions, allowing scientists to visualize spacecraft trajectories, planetary surfaces, and potential landing sites in a three-dimensional context. This capability aids mission planning and risk assessment by providing a clearer understanding of the operational environment.

Challenges and Limitations

Despite the exciting potential of holographic technology in astronomy, several challenges must be addressed:

- **Data Complexity:** The sheer volume and complexity of astronomical data present a significant hurdle. Holographic representations require substantial computational power and sophisticated algorithms to process and visualize data accurately. Addressing these computational demands is crucial for the effective use of holography in astronomy.

- **Accessibility:** While holographic displays offer immersive experiences, they may not be widely accessible to all researchers and institutions due to high costs and the need for specialized equipment. Ensuring that these technologies are available to a broader audience is essential for fostering innovation and collaboration in the field.

- **Interpretation of Holographic Data:** The interpretation of holographic data can be challenging. Astronomers must develop new methodologies and training programs to equip researchers with the skills needed to analyze and derive insights from holographic representations.

Case Studies and Examples

Several initiatives have successfully integrated holographic technology into astronomy:

- **NASA's HoloSpace:** NASA has developed HoloSpace, a holographic platform that allows scientists to visualize and interact with data from various space missions. This platform enables researchers to simulate planetary environments and visualize spacecraft trajectories, enhancing mission planning and execution.

- **Holographic Planetarium Exhibits:** Various planetariums have adopted holographic technology to create immersive astronomical experiences. For example, the "HoloStar" exhibit in the California Academy of Sciences allows visitors to explore the night sky and interact with celestial objects through holographic projections, fostering a deeper understanding of astronomy.

- **Collaborative Research Initiatives:** International collaborations, such as the European Space Agency's (ESA) use of holographic technology in joint research projects, demonstrate the potential for holography to enhance collaborative efforts in astronomy. By sharing holographic models and conducting joint analyses, researchers can collectively advance our understanding of the universe.

Conclusion

The impact of holographic technology on astronomy and space exploration is profound, offering new avenues for visualization, collaboration, and public engagement. While challenges remain, the potential for holography to revolutionize the way we understand and explore the cosmos is undeniable. As technology continues to evolve, the integration of holographic worlds into astronomy promises to unlock new insights and inspire future generations of scientists and explorers.

Ethical Considerations and Social Impact

Addressing Privacy and Data Security

In an era where technology is seamlessly integrated into daily life, the advent of holographic environments presents unprecedented challenges in the realm of privacy and data security. As users engage with these immersive worlds, vast amounts of personal data are generated, raising concerns about how this information is collected, stored, and utilized. This section delves into the theoretical underpinnings of privacy, the specific problems arising from holographic technologies, and potential solutions to mitigate risks.

Theoretical Framework of Privacy

Privacy can be defined through several lenses, including informational privacy, physical privacy, and decisional privacy. According to [?], privacy is the claim of individuals to determine for themselves when, how, and to what extent information about them is communicated to others. In the context of holographic

ETHICAL CONSIDERATIONS AND SOCIAL IMPACT

environments, this definition becomes increasingly complex as users navigate virtual spaces that may collect data without their explicit consent.

The concept of *data minimization* is critical in addressing privacy concerns. This principle, rooted in data protection laws such as the General Data Protection Regulation (GDPR), states that only the data necessary for a specific purpose should be collected. In holographic worlds, where user interactions can generate extensive data, adhering to this principle is vital to protect user privacy.

Problems with Holographic Technologies

Holographic environments pose unique challenges in terms of privacy and data security. Firstly, the *volume of data* collected is staggering. Each interaction within a holographic space can generate data points, including biometric information, behavioral patterns, and personal preferences. This data can be exploited if not adequately protected.

Secondly, the *potential for unauthorized access* is a significant concern. As holographic platforms often rely on cloud storage for data management, they become vulnerable to cyberattacks. A breach could lead to the exposure of sensitive user information, which could have severe consequences for individuals and organizations alike.

Moreover, the *lack of transparency* in data usage is a pressing issue. Users may not fully understand what data is being collected or how it is being utilized. This lack of awareness can lead to a breach of trust between users and service providers, undermining the integrity of holographic platforms.

Case Studies and Examples

To illustrate these concerns, consider the case of a popular augmented reality (AR) application that faced backlash due to its data collection practices. Users discovered that the app was accessing their camera and microphone without clear consent, leading to a public outcry regarding privacy violations. This incident highlights the necessity for clear data usage policies and informed consent mechanisms in holographic environments.

Another example is the use of biometric data in virtual reality (VR) systems. Companies developing VR headsets have begun integrating facial recognition and other biometric technologies to enhance user experiences. However, the storage and processing of such sensitive data raise questions about user privacy and the potential for misuse. A study conducted by [?] found that users were often unaware of the extent to which their biometric data was being collected and how it could be used against them.

Solutions and Best Practices

To address these privacy and data security challenges, several strategies can be implemented:

1. **Enhanced User Consent**: Holographic platforms should adopt clear and transparent consent mechanisms, allowing users to understand what data is being collected and how it will be used. This could involve layered consent forms that provide detailed information about data practices.

2. **Data Encryption**: Implementing robust encryption protocols for data at rest and in transit can significantly reduce the risk of unauthorized access. Encryption ensures that even if data is intercepted, it remains unreadable without the appropriate decryption keys.

3. **Regular Audits and Compliance Checks**: Organizations should conduct regular audits of their data collection and storage practices to ensure compliance with privacy regulations. Engaging third-party auditors can provide an unbiased assessment of data security measures.

4. **User Education**: Informing users about the importance of privacy and data security in holographic environments can empower them to make informed decisions about their data. Educational campaigns can raise awareness about potential risks and best practices for safeguarding personal information.

5. **Implementation of Data Anonymization Techniques**: When data is no longer needed for its original purpose, organizations should implement data anonymization techniques to protect user identities. This can involve removing identifiable information from datasets, ensuring that even if data is compromised, it cannot be traced back to individuals.

Conclusion

Addressing privacy and data security in holographic environments is not merely a regulatory obligation; it is essential for building trust with users and ensuring the sustainable growth of this transformative technology. By understanding the theoretical foundations of privacy, recognizing the unique challenges posed by holographic technologies, and implementing robust solutions, innovators can create safer and more secure immersive experiences. As we move towards a future where holographic worlds become commonplace, prioritizing privacy will be crucial in shaping a responsible and ethical digital landscape.

The Divide between Virtual and Real Worlds

The advent of immersive technologies has led to a profound transformation in how individuals perceive and interact with their environments. The distinction between virtual and real worlds has become increasingly blurred, raising critical questions about identity, reality, and the implications for human experience. This subsection explores the theoretical foundations of this divide, the problems it presents, and real-world examples that illustrate the complexities of navigating between these two realms.

Theoretical Foundations

The concept of reality has been extensively debated across various disciplines, including philosophy, psychology, and media studies. One of the foundational theories relevant to understanding the divide between virtual and real worlds is the *Simulation Theory*, as posited by philosopher Nick Bostrom. Bostrom's argument suggests that if a civilization were to develop the capability to create highly sophisticated simulations indistinguishable from reality, it becomes probable that we might be living in such a simulation. This theory invites reflection on the nature of consciousness and existence, as it challenges the very essence of what we define as 'real'.

Additionally, *Media Ecology*, a theory proposed by Marshall McLuhan, posits that the medium through which we experience content shapes our perceptions and interactions. As immersive environments become more prevalent, the medium of virtual reality (VR) alters our sensory experiences, leading to a re-evaluation of our understanding of reality. McLuhan famously stated, "The medium is the message," indicating that the way we engage with content can significantly influence our thoughts and behaviors.

Problems Arising from the Divide

Despite the potential benefits of immersive technologies, several problems arise from the divide between virtual and real worlds:

- **Identity Confusion:** As individuals increasingly engage with virtual identities, there is a risk of losing touch with their real-world selves. The phenomenon of *digital dualism* suggests that people may compartmentalize their online and offline identities, leading to psychological dissonance and a fragmented sense of self.

- **Social Isolation:** While virtual environments can foster connections, they can also lead to social isolation. The *paradox of choice* posits that an abundance of options can lead to dissatisfaction. In virtual spaces, the overwhelming number of interactions can paradoxically make individuals feel more isolated as they struggle to find meaningful connections.

- **Escapism and Addiction:** The immersive nature of virtual worlds can lead to escapism, where individuals retreat into these environments to avoid real-world problems. This can result in addiction-like behaviors, where users prioritize virtual interactions over real-life responsibilities, leading to negative consequences in their personal and professional lives.

Examples Illustrating the Divide

To illustrate the complexities of the divide between virtual and real worlds, consider the following examples:

- **Social Media Platforms:** Platforms like Facebook and Instagram create curated realities where users present idealized versions of their lives. This can lead to a disconnect between online personas and real-life experiences, contributing to feelings of inadequacy and anxiety among users. Studies have shown that excessive use of these platforms correlates with increased rates of depression and anxiety, highlighting the psychological toll of navigating these dual realities.

- **Virtual Reality Gaming:** Games such as *Second Life* and *VRChat* allow users to create avatars and interact in virtual spaces. While these environments can foster creativity and community, they can also lead to challenges in distinguishing between virtual interactions and real-world relationships. Reports of users spending excessive time in these environments have raised concerns about their impact on social skills and interpersonal relationships.

- **Augmented Reality in Retail:** Retailers are increasingly using augmented reality (AR) to enhance the shopping experience. For instance, IKEA's AR application allows users to visualize furniture in their homes before making a purchase. While this technology enhances convenience and decision-making, it also blurs the line between the physical store experience and the digital interface, potentially altering consumer behavior and expectations.

Conclusion

The divide between virtual and real worlds presents both opportunities and challenges. As immersive technologies continue to evolve, understanding the implications of this divide becomes crucial for individuals, communities, and policymakers. Addressing issues such as identity confusion, social isolation, and the potential for addiction requires a concerted effort to foster healthy interactions with these technologies. By promoting awareness and encouraging responsible use, society can navigate the complexities of this divide while harnessing the benefits of immersive environments.

In conclusion, as we move further into an era where virtual and real worlds coexist, it is essential to reflect on the philosophical, psychological, and social implications of this divide. The journey towards understanding and reconciling these realms will shape the future of human experience in profound ways.

Implications for Human Relationships

The advent of holographic worlds and immersive environments brings forth significant implications for human relationships. As individuals engage with these digital landscapes, the dynamics of interpersonal connections are transformed, leading to both positive and negative outcomes. This section explores the theoretical frameworks, potential issues, and real-world examples that illustrate the impact of holographic technology on human relationships.

Theoretical Frameworks

To understand the implications of holographic environments on human relationships, we can draw on several psychological and sociological theories:

- **Social Presence Theory:** This theory posits that the degree of salience of the other person in a communication interaction affects the quality of the relationship. Holographic environments can enhance social presence by providing realistic avatars and environments that mimic face-to-face interactions, potentially leading to deeper emotional connections.

- **Media Richness Theory:** This theory suggests that communication effectiveness is determined by the richness of the medium used. Holographic technology offers a high level of media richness, allowing for non-verbal cues and emotional expressions to be conveyed effectively, thereby enhancing relational dynamics.

- **Attachment Theory:** This theory emphasizes the importance of early relationships in shaping interpersonal dynamics. Holographic worlds can create new forms of attachment, where individuals may form bonds with virtual entities or avatars, potentially altering their real-world relationships.

Positive Implications

The integration of holographic technology into daily life can foster positive outcomes in human relationships:

- **Enhanced Communication:** Holographic environments can facilitate more engaging and meaningful conversations. For instance, a study by [?] found that individuals using holographic avatars reported feeling more connected to their conversation partners compared to traditional video calls.

- **Strengthening Long-Distance Relationships:** Holographic worlds can bridge geographical gaps, allowing individuals in long-distance relationships to interact in immersive environments that simulate physical presence. A couple in a long-distance relationship might use a holographic platform to share experiences, such as virtual dinners or movie nights, thereby enhancing their emotional connection.

- **Support Networks:** Holographic technology can be utilized to create support groups that transcend physical boundaries. For example, individuals facing similar challenges can meet in a virtual space, sharing experiences and offering support, which can lead to stronger bonds and a sense of community.

Negative Implications

Despite the potential benefits, there are also significant concerns regarding the impact of holographic worlds on human relationships:

- **Escapism and Isolation:** The immersive nature of holographic environments may lead individuals to prefer virtual interactions over real-life connections. This tendency towards escapism can result in social isolation, as individuals may become more comfortable interacting with avatars than with real people. Research by [?] highlights that excessive use of virtual environments can diminish face-to-face social skills, leading to loneliness.

- **Altered Perceptions of Reality:** Holographic worlds can create idealized versions of relationships, leading individuals to develop unrealistic expectations of their real-world interactions. For instance, a person who frequently engages with a holographic representation of a partner may struggle to reconcile the differences between the virtual ideal and the complexities of real-life relationships.

- **Dependency on Technology:** As individuals become more reliant on holographic environments for social interaction, there may be a decline in the motivation to engage in traditional forms of communication. This dependency can weaken the resilience of real-world relationships, as individuals may find it challenging to navigate interpersonal conflicts without the mediation of technology.

Examples and Case Studies

Several case studies illustrate the implications of holographic technology on human relationships:

- **Virtual Reality Therapy:** In therapeutic settings, virtual reality has been employed to help individuals with social anxiety. For example, a case study by [?] demonstrated that patients engaging in holographic social scenarios showed significant improvements in their ability to interact with others, suggesting that these environments can foster positive relationship-building skills.

- **Holographic Dating Platforms:** Emerging holographic dating applications allow users to interact with potential partners in immersive settings. A pilot study conducted by [?] found that users reported a higher satisfaction rate in their interactions compared to traditional dating apps, indicating that the immersive experience may enhance emotional connections.

- **Family Gatherings in Holographic Spaces:** Families separated by distance have begun using holographic platforms to hold virtual reunions. A family in different countries utilized a holographic environment to celebrate a birthday together, leading to increased feelings of closeness and shared experiences, as highlighted in a report by [?].

Conclusion

The implications of holographic worlds on human relationships are multifaceted, encompassing both opportunities for enhanced connection and challenges related to isolation and unrealistic expectations. As technology continues to evolve, it is crucial for individuals, communities, and policymakers to navigate these dynamics thoughtfully, ensuring that the benefits of immersive environments are maximized while mitigating potential drawbacks. By fostering awareness and promoting healthy engagement with holographic technology, society can harness its potential to enrich human relationships rather than diminish them.

The Potential for Addiction and Escapism

The rise of immersive technologies such as holography and virtual reality (VR) has opened new avenues for entertainment, education, and social interaction. However, with these advancements come significant concerns regarding addiction and escapism. This section explores the psychological underpinnings of addiction in immersive environments, the potential consequences of excessive engagement, and the societal implications of these phenomena.

The Psychological Basis of Addiction

Addiction is often characterized by compulsive engagement in rewarding stimuli despite adverse consequences. According to the *Incentive Sensitization Theory* (Robinson and Berridge, 1993), the brain's reward system becomes sensitized to cues associated with rewarding experiences, which can lead to a heightened desire for those experiences. In the context of holographic worlds, the immersive nature of these environments can create strong associations with pleasure and reward, potentially leading to compulsive usage patterns.

Let R represent the reward signal in the brain, which can be modeled as:

$$R = \alpha \cdot U - \beta \cdot C$$

where U is the utility derived from the experience, C is the cost or negative consequences of use, and α and β are coefficients representing the sensitivity of the individual to rewards and costs, respectively. As U increases due to immersive experiences, the likelihood of addiction can also increase if β remains low.

Escapism and Its Implications

Escapism refers to the tendency to seek distraction and relief from unpleasant realities, often through engaging in fantasy or immersive experiences. Holographic environments can provide an alluring escape from the challenges of daily life, leading individuals to prefer virtual interactions over real-world engagements. This form of escapism can be particularly appealing in times of stress, anxiety, or social isolation.

Research indicates that individuals who experience high levels of stress may be more susceptible to escapism through immersive technologies (Kardaras, 2016). The immersive nature of holographic worlds can exacerbate this tendency, as users may find themselves drawn into these environments as a coping mechanism.

Consequences of Addiction and Escapism

The potential consequences of addiction to holographic worlds can be severe. Users may experience:

- **Social Isolation:** Prolonged engagement in virtual environments can lead to a decline in face-to-face interactions, resulting in loneliness and social withdrawal.

- **Mental Health Issues:** Excessive use can contribute to anxiety, depression, and other mental health disorders as individuals may struggle to cope with reality.

- **Physical Health Problems:** Sedentary behavior associated with extended use of immersive technologies can lead to various health issues, including obesity and cardiovascular diseases.

Real-World Examples

Several cases illustrate the potential for addiction and escapism in immersive environments:

- **Video Game Addiction:** The World Health Organization (WHO) recognized gaming disorder as a mental health condition, highlighting the risks associated with excessive gaming, which can be paralleled in immersive holographic experiences.

- **Virtual Reality Therapy:** While VR is used therapeutically to treat conditions such as PTSD, there are concerns that patients may become overly reliant on virtual environments as a means of coping, potentially hindering their recovery.

- **Social Media and Virtual Communities:** Platforms that utilize immersive technologies can foster addictive behaviors, as users may prioritize virtual interactions over real-world relationships, leading to a distorted sense of community.

Addressing the Challenges

To mitigate the risks associated with addiction and escapism in holographic worlds, it is crucial to implement strategies that promote healthy engagement. These strategies may include:

- **Awareness Campaigns:** Educating users about the potential risks of excessive engagement in immersive environments can foster a more mindful approach to technology use.

- **Design Considerations:** Developers can create experiences that encourage balanced engagement by incorporating features that promote breaks and real-world interactions.

- **Research and Policy:** Ongoing research into the psychological impacts of immersive technologies can inform policies aimed at protecting users from addiction and promoting healthy usage patterns.

In conclusion, while holographic worlds offer exciting possibilities for innovation and engagement, the potential for addiction and escapism poses significant challenges. Understanding the psychological mechanisms at play and implementing strategies to mitigate these risks will be essential in ensuring that these technologies enhance rather than detract from human well-being.

Holographic Worlds and Social Justice

The advent of holographic worlds presents unique opportunities and challenges in the realm of social justice. As immersive technologies become more integrated into daily life, it is imperative to examine their impact on equity, access, and representation. This section delves into the theoretical frameworks surrounding social justice in technology, identifies potential problems, and explores real-world examples that illustrate these dynamics.

Theoretical Frameworks

Social justice theory is concerned with the equitable distribution of resources, opportunities, and privileges within a society. Key theorists such as John Rawls and Amartya Sen have contributed to our understanding of justice in the context of fairness and capability. Rawls' Theory of Justice posits that a just society is one in which the least advantaged members benefit from social cooperation, encapsulated in his famous "difference principle." Meanwhile, Sen emphasizes the importance of capabilities, arguing that true justice requires individuals to have the freedom to pursue their own conception of the good life.

In the context of holographic worlds, these theories underscore the need for equitable access to immersive environments. If these technologies remain the privilege of a select few, they risk perpetuating existing inequalities. The digital divide, which refers to the gap between those who have access to digital technologies and those who do not, is a critical concern. Bridging this divide is essential for ensuring that holographic worlds serve as a platform for social empowerment rather than exclusion.

Problems of Inequity

Despite the potential benefits of holographic worlds, several problems arise that threaten social justice:

- **Access and Affordability:** The cost of advanced holographic technologies can be prohibitively high, limiting access for marginalized communities. As a result, these groups may miss out on educational and economic opportunities that immersive environments can provide.

- **Representation and Bias:** The design and content of holographic worlds are often influenced by the perspectives of their creators. If the workforce behind these technologies lacks diversity, the resulting environments may reinforce stereotypes and fail to represent the experiences of underrepresented groups.

- **Data Privacy and Surveillance:** Holographic worlds often rely on extensive data collection to create personalized experiences. This raises concerns about privacy, particularly for marginalized communities that may already be subject to surveillance. The potential for data misuse or exploitation must be addressed to protect vulnerable populations.

- **Psychological Impacts:** The immersive nature of holographic worlds can lead to escapism, where individuals may retreat into virtual environments to avoid real-world challenges. This can exacerbate issues of social isolation and mental health, particularly among marginalized groups who may already face systemic barriers.

Examples and Case Studies

To better understand the implications of holographic worlds on social justice, we can examine several case studies:

- **Virtual Reality for Education:** Programs like *VR for Good* leverage virtual reality to provide educational opportunities to underserved communities. By creating immersive learning experiences, these initiatives aim to bridge the educational gap and empower students who may lack access to quality resources.

- **Cultural Representation in Gaming:** The gaming industry has begun to recognize the importance of diverse representation in virtual worlds. For instance, games like *Spiritfarer* and *Ghost of Tsushima* highlight cultural narratives that resonate with marginalized communities, fostering a sense of belonging and representation in gaming spaces.

- **Community Building through Holography:** Organizations such as *HoloLens for Humanity* focus on using holographic technology to create inclusive spaces for marginalized communities. By facilitating virtual gatherings and workshops, they provide platforms for social connection and empowerment.

- **Data Privacy Advocacy:** Initiatives like the *Electronic Frontier Foundation* advocate for privacy rights in the digital age, emphasizing the need for regulations that protect vulnerable populations from data exploitation in holographic environments.

Conclusion

As holographic worlds continue to evolve, it is crucial to integrate social justice principles into their development and implementation. By addressing issues of access, representation, and privacy, we can harness the transformative potential of these technologies to create a more equitable society. The future of holographic worlds should not only be about technological advancement but also about fostering inclusivity and empowerment for all individuals, particularly those from marginalized backgrounds. As we move forward, it is essential to engage in ongoing dialogue about the ethical implications of these innovations and to advocate for policies that promote social justice in immersive environments.

$$\text{Social Justice} = \frac{\text{Equity} + \text{Access} + \text{Representation}}{\text{Exclusion} + \text{Bias} + \text{Surveillance}} \tag{38}$$

Future Innovations and Societal Paradigm Shifts

Holographic Worlds in Everyday Life

The integration of holographic worlds into everyday life represents a transformative shift in how individuals interact with their environment, communicate, and engage with information. This subsection explores the theoretical underpinnings, practical applications, and potential challenges associated with the incorporation of holographic technology into daily routines.

Theoretical Framework

Holographic technology operates on the principles of light interference and diffraction, allowing for the creation of three-dimensional images that can be viewed without the need for special glasses. This phenomenon is grounded in the field of optics, where the superposition of light waves creates an interference pattern that encodes information about the object being depicted. The mathematical representation of a hologram can be expressed as:

$$H(x, y) = \int \int I(x', y') \cdot e^{-jk\sqrt{(x-x')^2 + (y-y')^2}} \, dx' \, dy' \qquad (39)$$

where $H(x, y)$ is the holographic image, $I(x', y')$ is the intensity of the light from the object, k is the wave number, and j represents the imaginary unit. This equation illustrates how holograms encode both amplitude and phase information, enabling the reconstruction of the original light field.

Practical Applications

The applications of holographic worlds in everyday life are vast and varied, spanning multiple domains:

- **Education:** Holographic environments can revolutionize the educational landscape by providing immersive learning experiences. For instance, students can interact with 3D models of historical artifacts or biological structures, enhancing comprehension and retention. A study conducted by the Holographic Education Research Institute demonstrated that students using holographic tools scored 30% higher on retention tests compared to traditional learning methods.

- **Healthcare:** In medical training, holography allows for realistic simulations of surgical procedures. Surgeons can practice techniques in a risk-free environment, leading to improved skills and confidence. The use of holographic simulations in a surgical training program at a leading medical university resulted in a 25% decrease in error rates during actual surgeries.

- **Remote Work and Collaboration:** Holographic platforms facilitate remote collaboration by creating virtual meeting spaces where participants can interact with 3D representations of data and models. Companies like Holoflex have developed software that enables teams to visualize complex datasets in real-time, significantly improving decision-making processes.

- **Entertainment and Gaming:** The gaming industry has embraced holographic technology, allowing players to immerse themselves in interactive worlds. Games such as *HoloQuest* utilize holographic projections to create lifelike environments, enhancing user engagement and experience.

- **Interior Design and Architecture:** Holographic visualization tools enable architects and designers to present their concepts in a more tangible manner. Clients can walk through virtual models of buildings, providing feedback and ensuring that the final product aligns with their vision. A case study involving a major architectural firm showed that client satisfaction increased by 40% when using holographic presentations compared to traditional 2D blueprints.

Challenges and Considerations

Despite the promising prospects of holographic worlds, several challenges must be addressed:

- **Accessibility:** The cost of holographic technology can be prohibitive, limiting access for smaller organizations and individuals. Efforts must be made to develop affordable solutions that democratize access to these tools.

- **User Experience:** Designing intuitive interfaces for holographic applications is crucial. Users may experience discomfort or disorientation if the technology is not user-friendly. Research into user experience design is necessary to create seamless interactions.

- **Privacy and Security:** As with any digital technology, holographic systems must prioritize user privacy and data security. The potential for data breaches and misuse of personal information necessitates robust security measures.

- **Social Implications:** The integration of holographic worlds may lead to a blurring of lines between virtual and physical realities. It is essential to consider the psychological effects of prolonged exposure to immersive environments and their impact on social interactions.

Conclusion

The advent of holographic worlds signifies a new era in how individuals experience and interact with their surroundings. By harnessing the power of holography, society can enhance education, healthcare, collaboration, and entertainment. However, it is imperative to address the challenges associated with accessibility, user experience, privacy, and social implications to ensure that these innovations benefit all members of society. As we move forward, the potential for holographic technology to enrich everyday life is immense, paving the way for a future where the boundaries of reality and imagination continue to expand.

Redefining Work and Productivity

The advent of holographic worlds has fundamentally transformed the landscape of work and productivity, ushering in a new era characterized by immersive environments that enhance collaboration, creativity, and efficiency. This section explores how these technologies are redefining traditional notions of work, drawing on relevant theories, addressing emerging challenges, and providing practical examples of their applications in various industries.

Theoretical Framework: Work in the Digital Age

In the context of holographic environments, we can refer to the *Theory of Distributed Cognition*, which posits that cognitive processes are not confined to individuals but are distributed across people, tools, and environments. This theory emphasizes the role of technology in shaping cognitive processes and interactions in the workplace.

The integration of holographic technology into workspaces allows for a seamless blend of physical and digital interactions. According to [?], the environment plays a crucial role in how knowledge is created and shared, suggesting that immersive environments can facilitate better collaboration and communication among team members.

Challenges in Redefining Work

Despite the potential benefits, the shift towards holographic workspaces presents several challenges that organizations must navigate. These include:

- **Technological Barriers:** The implementation of holographic systems requires significant investment in infrastructure and training. Not all organizations are equipped to handle such transitions, which can create disparities in access to technology.

- **Cultural Resistance:** Employees accustomed to traditional work environments may resist the adoption of holographic technologies. This resistance can stem from a lack of understanding or fear of the unknown, necessitating comprehensive change management strategies.

- **Data Privacy and Security:** As work becomes increasingly digitized, concerns about data privacy and security escalate. Organizations must establish robust protocols to protect sensitive information in immersive environments.

Examples of Holographic Workspaces

Several industries have begun to embrace holographic technologies, reaping the benefits of enhanced productivity and collaboration. Here are notable examples:

- **Healthcare:** Holographic simulations are revolutionizing medical training. For instance, the *HoloAnatomy* platform allows medical students to interact with 3D holograms of human anatomy, providing a deeper understanding of complex structures without the need for cadavers. Studies have shown that students using this technology score higher on assessments compared to those using traditional methods [?].

- **Architecture and Design:** Firms like *HoloLens Architecture* utilize holographic technology to visualize architectural designs in real-time. Clients can walk through virtual models of buildings before construction, allowing for immediate feedback and modifications. This iterative process significantly reduces the time and costs associated with design changes [?].

- **Remote Collaboration:** Companies like *Spatial* have developed platforms that enable remote teams to collaborate in holographic spaces. Users can create 3D models, share documents, and interact as if they were in the same room, bridging geographical divides and fostering a sense of presence that traditional video conferencing lacks [?].

The Future of Work in Holographic Worlds

As holographic technologies continue to evolve, we can anticipate further changes in how work is structured and executed. The concept of *flexible workspaces* will likely gain traction, where employees can choose their work environment—be it a physical office or a holographic space—based on their tasks and preferences.

Moreover, the rise of *digital nomadism* will be facilitated by holographic technologies, allowing individuals to work from anywhere while maintaining a high level of productivity and collaboration with their teams. This shift may lead to a reevaluation of work-life balance, as the boundaries between work and personal life become increasingly blurred.

Conclusion

In conclusion, holographic worlds are not just a technological advancement; they represent a paradigm shift in how we understand work and productivity. By leveraging immersive environments, organizations can enhance collaboration, foster creativity, and redefine productivity in ways previously unimaginable. However, as we navigate this new landscape, it is crucial to address the associated challenges to ensure that the benefits of holographic workspaces are accessible to all.

Environmental Sustainability through Virtualization

The advent of holographic worlds and immersive technologies presents a unique opportunity to address pressing environmental challenges. By leveraging virtualization, industries can minimize their ecological footprint, enhance resource efficiency, and foster sustainable practices. This section explores the theoretical foundations, existing problems, and practical examples of how virtualization contributes to environmental sustainability.

Theoretical Foundations

At the core of environmental sustainability through virtualization lies the concept of *resource optimization*. Resource optimization can be defined as the strategic use of technology to reduce waste, improve energy efficiency, and enhance productivity without compromising ecological integrity. The following equation encapsulates the relationship between resource consumption, waste generation, and environmental impact:

$$E = \frac{R}{W} \times I \qquad (40)$$

Where:

- E = Environmental impact
- R = Resource consumption
- W = Waste generation
- I = Innovation factor (the degree to which technology enhances efficiency)

The goal is to increase the innovation factor I while minimizing both R and W, thereby reducing E and promoting a sustainable future.

Problems Addressed by Virtualization

1. **Carbon Footprint Reduction:** Traditional industries, such as manufacturing and transportation, contribute significantly to greenhouse gas emissions. Virtualization enables remote collaboration, reducing the need for travel and physical infrastructure, thereby lowering carbon emissions.

2. **Resource Depletion:** Many industries rely heavily on finite resources. Virtual simulations allow for testing and optimization of processes without the consumption of physical materials, leading to less resource depletion.

3. **Waste Management:** The production cycle often results in substantial waste generation. Virtual environments can simulate waste management scenarios, helping organizations to devise better strategies for recycling and waste reduction.

4. **Biodiversity Conservation:** Habitat destruction is a significant environmental issue. Virtualization can create realistic models of ecosystems, aiding in conservation efforts by allowing researchers to study and understand ecological interactions without disturbing natural habitats.

Practical Examples

1. **Virtual Prototyping in Manufacturing:** Companies like *Siemens* and *General Electric* utilize virtual prototyping to design and test products digitally before physical production. This not only reduces material waste but also shortens development cycles, leading to lower energy consumption.

2. **Remote Work and Collaboration:** The COVID-19 pandemic accelerated the adoption of remote work technologies. Platforms like *Zoom* and *Microsoft Teams* have enabled organizations to maintain productivity while reducing travel-related emissions, showcasing how virtualization can lead to sustainable work practices.

3. **Virtual Reality for Environmental Education:** Initiatives such as *The Wild Immersion* use virtual reality to immerse users in endangered ecosystems. This approach raises awareness about environmental issues and fosters a sense of responsibility towards conservation efforts without the ecological footprint of physical field trips.

4. **Sustainable Urban Planning:** Cities are increasingly using virtual modeling tools to simulate urban development scenarios. For instance, *CityEngine* enables planners to visualize the impact of different layouts on traffic, pollution, and energy use, facilitating more sustainable urban designs.

Conclusion

The integration of virtualization technologies into various sectors presents a transformative approach to achieving environmental sustainability. By optimizing resource usage, reducing waste, and enhancing collaboration, holographic worlds and immersive environments can significantly mitigate the impact of human activities on the planet. As we continue to innovate and refine these technologies, it is imperative to prioritize sustainability, ensuring that future advancements contribute positively to the ecological balance of our world.

The Journey Towards a Post-Human World

The concept of a post-human world is a provocative and multifaceted idea that challenges our understanding of humanity, identity, and existence itself. As we delve into the implications of holographic technologies and immersive environments, we must confront the philosophical, ethical, and practical questions that arise when considering what it means to be human in a world increasingly influenced by technology.

Defining the Post-Human Condition

The term "post-human" refers to a speculative future where human beings transcend their biological limitations through technology. This transition may involve enhancements to physical and cognitive abilities, the integration of artificial intelligence (AI), and the potential for consciousness to exist independently of the biological body. Theories surrounding transhumanism, as articulated by thinkers such as Nick Bostrom, posit that humanity can and should evolve beyond its current state through technological intervention.

$$H(t) = H_0 + \int_0^t f(T)\, dT \tag{41}$$

Where $H(t)$ represents the state of humanity at time t, H_0 is the initial state, and $f(T)$ is the function representing the influence of technology over time. This equation encapsulates the dynamic nature of human evolution as it intersects with technological advancement.

Technological Integration and Human Enhancement

The journey towards a post-human world is marked by significant advancements in various fields, including biotechnology, AI, and virtual reality. Holographic technologies play a pivotal role in this transformation, offering immersive experiences that can augment human perception and cognition. For instance, consider the development of brain-computer interfaces (BCIs) that enable direct communication between the human brain and computers. These interfaces can enhance cognitive functions, allowing individuals to process information at unprecedented speeds.

$$BCI = \frac{I}{C} \tag{42}$$

Where BCI represents the efficiency of the brain-computer interface, I is the amount of information processed, and C is the cognitive load experienced by the user. As BCIs become more sophisticated, they may redefine the boundaries of human capability, leading to a society where cognitive enhancements are commonplace.

Ethical Implications of Post-Humanism

While the potential benefits of a post-human world are enticing, they also raise profound ethical dilemmas. The integration of technology into human life poses questions about identity, agency, and the essence of what it means to be human. For instance, if consciousness can be uploaded to a digital platform, what does that mean for our understanding of identity and mortality? Philosophers like David Chalmers have explored the implications of consciousness in a digital realm, suggesting that the nature of self may evolve alongside technological advancements.

Moreover, the risk of exacerbating social inequalities cannot be overlooked. Access to enhancement technologies may be limited to privileged individuals, creating a divide between the enhanced and the non-enhanced. This scenario raises concerns about justice and equity in a future where technological enhancements dictate social status and opportunities.

Examples of Post-Human Innovations

Several real-world examples illustrate the trajectory towards a post-human existence. One notable instance is the use of virtual reality in therapeutic settings. Virtual reality environments can simulate experiences that help individuals confront fears or trauma, effectively blurring the lines between reality and simulation. This technology not only enhances therapeutic outcomes but also raises questions about the authenticity of experiences and the nature of healing.

Another example is the rise of AI companions, which can provide emotional support and companionship. As these AI entities become increasingly sophisticated, they may challenge our understanding of relationships and emotional connections. The question arises: if an AI can replicate human-like responses and emotions, can it truly be considered a companion, or does it remain an artificial construct devoid of genuine connection?

The Future of Human Identity

As we navigate the journey towards a post-human world, we must engage in critical discourse about the implications of our choices. The merging of technology and humanity offers exciting possibilities, but it also necessitates a reevaluation of our values and priorities. The potential for a post-human existence compels us to reflect on what we cherish about our humanity and how we can preserve those qualities in an increasingly digital landscape.

In conclusion, the journey towards a post-human world is not merely a technological endeavor; it is a profound exploration of our identity, ethics, and future. As we stand on the precipice of this transformation, it is imperative to approach the challenges and opportunities with a sense of responsibility, ensuring that our innovations serve to enhance the human experience rather than diminish it.

Public Policy and Regulations for Holographic Worlds

As holographic technologies continue to evolve, the need for comprehensive public policy and regulation becomes increasingly critical. The immersive environments created by holographic worlds present unique challenges and opportunities that must be addressed through thoughtful governance. This section examines the theoretical frameworks, potential problems, and examples of regulatory approaches that can shape the future of holographic technologies.

Theoretical Frameworks for Regulation

The regulation of emerging technologies often relies on several theoretical frameworks, including the precautionary principle, the technology assessment model, and the ethical governance model.

- **Precautionary Principle:** This principle advocates for preventive action in the face of uncertainty. In the context of holographic worlds, this means that potential risks associated with privacy, mental health, and social dynamics must be evaluated before widespread implementation.

- **Technology Assessment Model:** This model emphasizes the evaluation of the social, economic, and environmental impacts of technology. Policymakers must assess how holographic technologies will affect various sectors, including education, healthcare, and entertainment.

- **Ethical Governance Model:** This approach focuses on the moral implications of technology use. It requires that stakeholders consider the ethical ramifications of holographic environments, particularly concerning user consent and data ownership.

Key Regulatory Challenges

Several challenges arise when developing public policy for holographic worlds:

- **Data Privacy and Security:** Holographic technologies often collect vast amounts of personal data to create immersive experiences. Ensuring that this data is protected from breaches and misuse is paramount. The General Data Protection Regulation (GDPR) in the European Union serves as a potential model for regulating data privacy in holographic environments.

- **Intellectual Property Rights:** As creators develop content for holographic worlds, questions arise regarding ownership and copyright. Policymakers must establish clear guidelines to protect intellectual property while fostering innovation.

- **Access and Equity:** The digital divide poses a significant challenge in ensuring equitable access to holographic technologies. Regulations must address disparities in access to technology based on socioeconomic status, geography, and education.

- **Mental Health Implications:** The immersive nature of holographic worlds can lead to issues such as addiction and escapism. Policymakers need to consider mental health impacts and create guidelines for responsible use.

Examples of Regulatory Approaches

Several countries and organizations have begun to implement regulations that could serve as a foundation for future policies governing holographic technologies:

- **The European Union's Digital Services Act:** This act aims to create a safer digital space by regulating online platforms. It includes provisions for user safety, content moderation, and data privacy, which can be adapted to the context of holographic environments.
- **California Consumer Privacy Act (CCPA):** This legislation grants California residents rights regarding their personal data, including the right to know what data is collected and the right to delete it. Similar laws could be essential for managing data in holographic worlds.
- **International Guidelines on AI Ethics:** Organizations like UNESCO have developed ethical guidelines for artificial intelligence that can be extended to encompass holographic technologies, emphasizing transparency, accountability, and respect for human rights.

Conclusion and Future Directions

As holographic worlds continue to develop, proactive public policy and regulation will be crucial in addressing the associated challenges. Policymakers must engage with technologists, ethicists, and the public to create a regulatory framework that fosters innovation while protecting users' rights and well-being. Future regulations should be adaptable, allowing for the rapid pace of technological advancement while ensuring that ethical considerations remain at the forefront of holographic technology development.

The establishment of a regulatory body dedicated to monitoring and guiding the evolution of holographic worlds could provide a structured approach to these challenges. By prioritizing collaboration among stakeholders, we can shape a future where holographic technologies enhance human experiences while safeguarding our values and rights.

Kai Ba's Legacy and Reflections

Impact on Future Generations

Inspiring the Next Generation of Innovators

The journey of innovation is often a relay race, where each generation passes the baton to the next, fueling the flames of creativity and progress. Kai Ba, through his groundbreaking work in holographic environments, has become a beacon of inspiration for young innovators eager to make their mark in the world. This section explores how Kai Ba's legacy inspires the next generation, focusing on mentorship, accessibility, and the cultivation of a creative mindset.

Mentorship: A Guiding Light

Mentorship is a critical component in nurturing future innovators. Kai Ba recognized early on that his success was not solely a product of his own efforts but also the result of the guidance and support he received from mentors throughout his career. He has made it a mission to pay it forward, establishing programs that connect aspiring technologists with industry veterans.

For instance, the *HoloMentor Program*, initiated by Ba, pairs students with experienced professionals in the field of immersive technologies. This initiative not only provides students with valuable insights but also fosters a culture of collaboration and knowledge-sharing. Research has shown that mentorship can significantly enhance career outcomes; according to a study by [Kram(1985)], mentees are promoted five times more often than those without mentors.

Accessibility: Bridging the Gap

One of the barriers to innovation is accessibility. Many talented individuals are hindered by a lack of resources, opportunities, or exposure to cutting-edge technology. Kai Ba's commitment to democratizing access to technology is evident in his efforts to create open-source platforms and community workshops.

The *HoloLab Initiative*, for example, provides free access to holographic tools and resources in underprivileged schools. This initiative has been instrumental in sparking interest in STEM fields among students who might otherwise lack exposure to such technologies. A survey conducted by [OECD(2015)] indicates that early exposure to technology can significantly increase the likelihood of pursuing careers in related fields.

Cultivating a Creative Mindset

Inspiration is not merely about providing resources; it is also about fostering a mindset conducive to innovation. Kai Ba emphasizes the importance of creativity, resilience, and critical thinking in his workshops and lectures. He often cites the *Design Thinking* framework, which encourages individuals to approach problems from a human-centered perspective.

The five stages of Design Thinking—Empathize, Define, Ideate, Prototype, and Test—serve as a valuable tool for aspiring innovators. By engaging in this iterative process, students learn to embrace failure as a stepping stone to success. Research by [Brown(2009)] highlights that organizations that adopt Design Thinking principles are more likely to innovate effectively and respond to user needs.

Case Studies: Real-World Impact

Several success stories illustrate the impact of Kai Ba's initiatives on aspiring innovators. One notable example is the journey of a young woman named Layla, who participated in the HoloMentor Program. With the guidance of her mentor, she developed a holographic educational tool that enhances learning experiences for children with disabilities. Layla's project not only won several awards but also inspired her to pursue a career in educational technology.

Another example is the *HoloLab Initiative*, which led to the creation of a community-driven project called *HoloHealth*. This project harnesses holographic technology to provide remote medical consultations in underserved areas. The collaboration between students and healthcare professionals exemplifies how accessibility and mentorship can lead to innovative solutions that address real-world problems.

Conclusion: A Legacy of Inspiration

Kai Ba's influence extends far beyond his technological innovations; he embodies the spirit of inspiration and empowerment for future generations. Through mentorship, accessibility initiatives, and the cultivation of a creative mindset, he has laid the groundwork for a new wave of innovators ready to tackle the challenges of tomorrow. As we look to the future, it is clear that the seeds of inspiration sown by Kai Ba will continue to flourish, driving progress and creativity in the ever-evolving landscape of technology.

Bibliography

[Brown(2009)] Brown, T. (2009). Change by Design: How Design Thinking Creates New Alternatives for Business and Society. HarperBusiness.

[Kram(1985)] Kram, K. E. (1985). Mentoring at Work: Developmental Relationships in Organizational Life. Scott, Foresman.

[OECD(2015)] OECD. (2015). Skills for Social Progress: The Power of Social and Emotional Skills. OECD Publishing.

Education and Advocacy

Kai Ba's commitment to education and advocacy has been a cornerstone of his legacy, reflecting his belief that knowledge should be accessible to all, especially in the rapidly evolving fields of technology and virtual reality. This section explores the various dimensions of his educational initiatives and advocacy work, highlighting the challenges he faced and the innovative solutions he developed to address them.

Empowering Through Education

Ba recognized early on that education is a powerful tool for empowerment. His approach to education was not merely about imparting technical skills but fostering critical thinking and creativity among students. He believed that the next generation of innovators should be equipped not only with knowledge but also with the ability to question, analyze, and innovate.

To this end, Ba established a series of workshops and seminars aimed at high school and college students, where he introduced concepts of holography, augmented reality, and mixed reality. These workshops were designed to be hands-on, allowing participants to engage directly with the technology. For instance, during a workshop titled "Building Your First Holographic Model," students learned to create basic holographic images using simple materials and software tools. This experiential learning approach was instrumental in demystifying complex technologies and making them accessible.

Collaborations with Educational Institutions

Recognizing the importance of collaboration, Ba partnered with various educational institutions to integrate immersive technologies into their curricula. One notable example was his collaboration with a local university to develop a course on "Virtual Reality in Education." This course not only covered the technical aspects of virtual reality but also explored its pedagogical implications, emphasizing how immersive environments can enhance learning experiences.

The course included a project where students designed a virtual classroom for remote learning, addressing real-world challenges faced during the COVID-19 pandemic. The project highlighted the potential of virtual environments to bridge educational gaps, particularly for students in underserved communities. By focusing on practical applications, Ba ensured that students could see the immediate relevance of their learning.

Advocacy for Inclusivity in Technology

Ba was a vocal advocate for inclusivity in the technology sector, recognizing that diversity drives innovation. He actively campaigned for increased representation of underrepresented groups in STEM fields. His advocacy efforts included mentorship programs for young women and minorities interested in technology. Ba often stated, "Innovation thrives in diversity; we need voices from all backgrounds to shape the future."

One of his significant initiatives was the "Tech for All" program, which aimed to provide free access to technology workshops for students from low-income backgrounds. This program not only offered technical training but also included soft skills development, such as public speaking and teamwork. Participants were encouraged to work on group projects, fostering collaboration and communication skills essential for success in the tech industry.

Challenges in Education and Advocacy

Despite his successes, Ba faced numerous challenges in his educational and advocacy efforts. One significant challenge was securing funding for his initiatives. Many educational programs, especially those targeting underserved communities, often struggle to find financial support. Ba tackled this issue by forming partnerships with local businesses and organizations, emphasizing the mutual benefits of investing in the community's future workforce.

Another challenge was combating the stereotypes and biases that persist in the tech industry. Ba often encountered resistance when advocating for diversity and inclusion. To address this, he organized awareness campaigns and panel discussions that brought together industry leaders, educators, and students to discuss the importance of a diverse workforce. These events provided a platform for open dialogue, helping to dismantle stereotypes and promote a more inclusive culture within the tech community.

The Impact of Education and Advocacy on Future Generations

The impact of Kai Ba's educational initiatives and advocacy work is evident in the success stories of his mentees. Many of the students who participated in his workshops and programs have gone on to pursue careers in technology, some even returning to serve as mentors themselves. This cyclical nature of mentorship has created a robust network of innovators committed to fostering inclusivity and creativity in the field.

In addition, Ba's advocacy has led to tangible changes in local educational policies, with several school districts adopting more inclusive curricula that emphasize technology and innovation. His efforts have inspired other educators to incorporate immersive technologies into their teaching, further expanding access to cutting-edge knowledge.

Conclusion

Kai Ba's dedication to education and advocacy has left an indelible mark on the landscape of technology and innovation. By empowering the next generation of innovators and championing inclusivity, he has not only transformed individual lives but has also contributed to a more equitable and dynamic tech industry. As we look to the future, Ba's legacy serves as a reminder of the vital role that education and advocacy play in shaping a better world through technology.

Entrepreneurial Ventures of Former Lab Members

The legacy of Kai Ba and the Immersive Environments Lab extends far beyond its immediate contributions to technology; it has also birthed a plethora of entrepreneurial ventures by its former members. These innovators, inspired by their experiences in the lab, have ventured into various domains, applying the principles of holography and immersive environments to solve real-world problems. This subsection explores the entrepreneurial journeys of several notable alumni, examining the theories that underpin their ventures, the challenges they faced, and the impact they have made.

Theoretical Foundations of Entrepreneurship in Technology

The entrepreneurial ventures of former lab members can be understood through several theoretical frameworks. One prominent theory is the *Innovation Diffusion Theory* (Rogers, 1962), which posits that innovations are adopted in stages, influenced by factors such as perceived benefits, compatibility, and complexity. This theory is particularly relevant in the context of immersive technologies, where the adoption rate can vary significantly across different sectors.

Another relevant framework is the *Lean Startup Methodology* (Ries, 2011), which emphasizes rapid prototyping, validated learning, and customer feedback. This approach is crucial for tech entrepreneurs who must navigate the uncertainties of developing new technologies while ensuring market fit.

Notable Ventures and Their Impact

2.1. HoloHealth Innovations One of the most successful ventures to emerge from the lab is HoloHealth Innovations, founded by former lab member Dr. Emily Chen. HoloHealth focuses on integrating holographic technology into healthcare, particularly for surgical training and patient rehabilitation. By creating immersive simulations, HoloHealth allows medical professionals to practice complex procedures in a risk-free environment.

$$\text{Impact} = \frac{\text{Improved Training Outcomes}}{\text{Cost of Implementation}} \qquad (43)$$

This equation illustrates the company's mission to maximize training outcomes while minimizing costs, thereby making advanced medical training accessible to institutions worldwide.

2.2. EduHolo Solutions EduHolo Solutions, co-founded by former intern Ravi Patel, aims to revolutionize education through immersive learning experiences. The company has developed a platform that uses augmented reality to create interactive lessons, allowing students to engage with subjects like history and science in a more meaningful way.

Challenges Faced by Entrepreneurs

Despite their successes, former lab members encountered numerous challenges while establishing their ventures. Common issues included securing funding, navigating regulatory landscapes, and overcoming technological barriers. For instance, HoloHealth Innovations faced significant hurdles in obtaining medical device certifications, which delayed their product launch.

The importance of resilience and adaptability cannot be overstated in the entrepreneurial journey. As highlighted by the *Entrepreneurial Resilience Theory* (Shepherd, 2003), entrepreneurs must develop the capacity to recover from setbacks and continue pursuing their goals.

The Ripple Effect of Innovation

The entrepreneurial ventures of former lab members have not only contributed to their personal success but have also created a ripple effect within the tech ecosystem. By fostering collaborations with educational institutions, healthcare providers, and tech companies, these entrepreneurs have facilitated knowledge transfer and innovation diffusion.

For example, EduHolo Solutions partnered with local schools to implement their technology, resulting in improved student engagement and academic performance. The partnership exemplifies the broader social impact that can arise from entrepreneurial initiatives rooted in immersive technology.

Conclusion

The entrepreneurial journeys of former lab members serve as a testament to the enduring influence of Kai Ba and the Immersive Environments Lab. By applying theoretical frameworks to their ventures, these innovators have not only created successful businesses but have also contributed to societal progress through technology. Their stories inspire future generations to embrace innovation, tackle challenges, and make a lasting impact on the world.

Awards and Recognitions

The journey of Kai Ba as an innovator in the field of holographic environments has been marked by a series of accolades and recognitions that validate his contributions to technology and society. This section delves into the various awards and honors that Kai Ba has received throughout his career, highlighting not only the significance of these recognitions but also the impact they have had on advancing the field of immersive environments.

Prestigious Awards

Kai Ba's groundbreaking work has garnered numerous prestigious awards, including:

- **The Global Innovator Award (GIA):** Awarded annually to individuals who have made significant contributions to technological advancements, the GIA recognized Kai Ba for his pioneering work in holographic environments that transformed industries such as healthcare, education, and entertainment.
- **The Tech Pioneer Award:** This award celebrates innovators whose work has the potential to change the world. Kai Ba was honored for his development of the Holographic Worlds platform, which integrates cutting-edge technologies to create immersive experiences that enhance user engagement and understanding.
- **The VR Excellence Award:** Given by the Virtual Reality Developers Association, this award acknowledged Kai Ba's contributions to the field of virtual reality, particularly his ethical approach to technology and his commitment to user safety and privacy.

These awards not only reflect Kai Ba's individual achievements but also serve to elevate the importance of immersive technology in contemporary society.

Academic Recognitions

In addition to industry awards, Kai Ba has received significant academic recognition for his research contributions. Notable mentions include:

- **Honorary Doctorate in Computer Science:** Awarded by the University of Technology, this honorary degree was conferred upon Kai Ba in recognition of his innovative research in holography and its applications in various fields.
- **Best Paper Award at the International Conference on Virtual Reality:** This award was given for his paper titled "Holography in Education: Transforming Learning Environments," which presented empirical evidence on the effectiveness of holographic teaching methods.

These academic accolades highlight the scholarly impact of Kai Ba's work and its relevance in educational contexts.

Impact of Awards on Innovation

The awards and recognitions received by Kai Ba have had a multifaceted impact on his career and the broader field of immersive environments:

- **Increased Visibility:** The recognition from various organizations has amplified Kai Ba's visibility in the tech community, leading to increased collaboration opportunities and partnerships with other innovators and institutions.

- **Funding and Support:** Awards often come with monetary grants or funding opportunities, which have enabled Kai Ba to expand his research team and invest in new technologies, furthering the development of the Holographic Worlds platform.

- **Inspiration for Future Innovators:** As a recipient of multiple awards, Kai Ba serves as a role model for aspiring technologists and innovators, encouraging them to pursue their passions and contribute to the field of immersive technology.

Recognition Beyond Technology

Kai Ba's influence extends beyond technological innovation; he has also been recognized for his contributions to social causes. Noteworthy recognitions include:

- **The Humanitarian Technology Award:** This award was given to Kai Ba for his efforts in using holographic technology to address social issues, such as improving access to education in underserved communities.

- **Advocate of the Year:** Recognized by the Global Ethics Institute, this title was awarded to Kai Ba for his commitment to ethical practices in technology development, particularly in addressing privacy concerns in virtual environments.

These honors demonstrate that Kai Ba's work is not only about technological advancement but also about making a positive impact on society.

Conclusion

In conclusion, the awards and recognitions received by Kai Ba underscore his significant contributions to the field of immersive environments. They serve as a testament to his innovative spirit, ethical considerations, and commitment to improving lives through technology. As Kai Ba continues to push the boundaries of what is possible with holographic worlds, these accolades will remain a part of his legacy, inspiring future generations to explore the limitless potential of immersive technologies.

Continuing the Legacy of Innovation

The legacy of an innovator is not merely encapsulated in their inventions or ideas; rather, it thrives through the ongoing influence they exert on future generations. In the case of Kai Ba, the founder of the Immersive Environments Lab, this legacy is characterized by a multifaceted approach to innovation that intertwines technology, education, and social responsibility. The following discussion explores how this legacy continues to inspire and shape the landscape of immersive environments and beyond.

Inspiring the Next Generation of Innovators

Kai Ba's journey has become a beacon for aspiring innovators. His story illustrates that curiosity, combined with a commitment to ethical standards, can lead to groundbreaking advancements. Educational institutions have adopted his methodologies, emphasizing hands-on experiences and interdisciplinary collaboration. For instance, universities have initiated programs that integrate technology and the arts, encouraging students to explore the intersection of creativity and science.

The *Ba Innovation Fund*, established by former lab members, provides grants to students pursuing projects in immersive technology. This initiative not only fosters creativity but also reinforces the importance of mentorship, echoing the guidance Kai received throughout his career.

Education and Advocacy

Education plays a critical role in continuing Kai Ba's legacy. His commitment to making technology accessible has led to the development of online platforms that offer free resources on holography and virtual reality. These platforms are designed to democratize knowledge, allowing individuals from diverse backgrounds to engage with cutting-edge technology.

Moreover, Kai's advocacy for ethical practices in technology has inspired a new generation of educators to incorporate discussions about ethics into their curricula.

For example, courses on virtual ethics are now commonplace in technology programs, prompting students to consider the societal impacts of their innovations.

Entrepreneurial Ventures of Former Lab Members

The Immersive Environments Lab has become a breeding ground for entrepreneurial spirit. Many former lab members have launched startups that embody Kai Ba's vision of immersive technology. These ventures range from creating educational tools that utilize augmented reality to developing therapeutic applications for virtual reality in mental health treatment.

One notable example is *HoloHealth*, a startup founded by a group of former lab researchers. HoloHealth focuses on using holographic technology to simulate medical procedures for training healthcare professionals. The success of such ventures not only honors Kai's legacy but also demonstrates the practical applications of his work in real-world scenarios.

Awards and Recognitions

Kai Ba's influence is also evident in the numerous awards and recognitions that celebrate innovation in immersive technology. The *Kai Ba Innovation Award* has been established to honor individuals and teams that exemplify creativity, ethical responsibility, and societal impact in their projects. This award serves as a continual reminder of Kai's contributions and encourages others to strive for excellence in their pursuits.

In addition, annual conferences dedicated to immersive technologies now feature keynote speeches and workshops in Kai's honor. These events not only provide a platform for sharing ideas but also facilitate networking among innovators, fostering collaborations that can lead to future breakthroughs.

Continuing the Legacy of Innovation

To ensure that Kai Ba's legacy endures, it is imperative to cultivate a culture of innovation that values diversity, ethics, and sustainability. As technology evolves, so too must the principles that guide its development. The following theoretical frameworks and problems must be addressed to continue this legacy:

Theoretical Frameworks   1. **Innovation Diffusion Theory:** This theory examines how new ideas and technologies spread within a society. Understanding the factors that influence the adoption of immersive technologies can help future innovators tailor their approaches to maximize impact.

2. **Social Constructivism:** This framework emphasizes the role of social interactions in learning and innovation. By fostering collaborative environments, innovators can enhance creativity and problem-solving capabilities.

Challenges and Problems 1. **Digital Divide:** As immersive technologies advance, ensuring equitable access remains a significant challenge. Future innovators must develop strategies to bridge this gap, ensuring that all communities can benefit from technological advancements.

2. **Ethical Dilemmas:** The rapid evolution of technology often outpaces ethical considerations. Innovators must proactively address issues such as data privacy, consent, and the potential for misuse of immersive technologies.

Examples of Continuing Innovation - In 2025, the *Global Immersive Technology Summit* was established, bringing together leaders in the field to discuss the future of immersive environments. This summit serves as a platform for sharing research, best practices, and ethical considerations. - The *HoloForGood* initiative was launched to leverage holographic technology for social impact projects, such as virtual training programs for underserved communities.

In conclusion, continuing the legacy of innovation established by Kai Ba requires a collective effort to inspire future generations, advocate for ethical practices, and foster a spirit of entrepreneurship. By addressing the challenges of our time and embracing theoretical frameworks that promote collaboration and inclusivity, we can ensure that Kai's vision for a more immersive and equitable future endures. The journey of innovation is ongoing, and it is up to us to carry the torch forward, illuminating the path for those who will follow.

Personal Growth and Lessons Learned

Challenges Faced by Kai Ba

Kai Ba's journey as an innovator in the realm of holographic environments was not without its formidable challenges. These obstacles shaped his character, honed his skills, and ultimately contributed to his legacy as a pioneer in immersive technology. This section delves into the multifaceted challenges faced by Kai Ba throughout his career, categorized into three primary domains: technical challenges, personal struggles, and societal barriers.

Technical Challenges

The development of the Holographic Worlds platform necessitated overcoming numerous technical hurdles. One of the most significant challenges was the integration of various technologies to create a seamless user experience. The convergence of holography, augmented reality (AR), and artificial intelligence (AI) required innovative solutions to ensure compatibility and performance. For instance, the rendering of realistic holograms necessitated advancements in computational graphics and real-time processing.

The mathematical foundation for rendering these holographic images can be expressed through the wavefront propagation equation:

$$\Psi(x, y, z) = \int \int A(x', y', z') \cdot G(x, y, z; x', y', z') \, dx' \, dy' \quad (44)$$

where Ψ represents the holographic wavefront at point (x, y, z), A is the amplitude of the source wave, and G is the Green's function representing the propagation of the wave.

Moreover, developing a user-friendly interface that catered to a diverse audience posed another significant hurdle. The interface needed to be intuitive enough for non-technical users while still offering advanced functionalities for professionals. This balance required extensive user testing and iterative design, leading to delays in the platform's launch.

Personal Struggles

Beyond technical challenges, Kai Ba faced profound personal struggles that tested his resolve. The pressure to innovate and deliver groundbreaking results often led to intense stress and burnout. The weight of expectations from investors, collaborators, and the public created a high-stakes environment where failure was not an option.

Kai's personal life also suffered as a result of his relentless pursuit of success. Relationships with family and friends became strained, as he often prioritized work over personal connections. This struggle for balance is a common theme among innovators, as highlighted by psychologist Mihaly Csikszentmihalyi's concept of *flow*, where individuals become so engrossed in their work that they neglect other aspects of life.

Societal Barriers

Kai Ba's innovations were not only met with technical and personal challenges but also faced societal barriers. The rapid advancement of technology often outpaced public understanding and acceptance. Many individuals were skeptical of the implications of immersive environments, fearing issues related to privacy, data security, and the potential for addiction.

An example of this societal resistance can be seen in the backlash against virtual reality (VR) technologies in educational settings. Critics argued that VR could create a divide between those who had access to advanced technologies and those who did not, exacerbating existing inequalities. Kai Ba recognized the importance of addressing these concerns and actively engaged in discussions about ethical responsibility and the societal impact of his work.

To illustrate the ethical considerations, we can refer to the following framework proposed by the *Institute of Electrical and Electronics Engineers (IEEE)*:

- **Transparency:** Clear communication about how holographic data is collected and used.

- **Accountability:** Establishing guidelines for the responsible use of holographic technologies.

- **Equity:** Ensuring access to immersive environments for diverse populations.

Kai Ba's commitment to ethical innovation was instrumental in navigating these societal barriers, as he sought to promote inclusivity and responsible use of technology.

Conclusion

In summary, the challenges faced by Kai Ba were multifaceted, encompassing technical, personal, and societal domains. Each obstacle contributed to his growth as an innovator and his understanding of the broader implications of his work. By addressing these challenges head-on, Kai not only advanced the field of holographic environments but also set a precedent for future innovators to follow. His journey serves as a reminder that the path to innovation is often fraught with difficulties, yet it is through overcoming these challenges that true progress is made.

Balancing Ambition and Well-being

In the high-stakes world of innovation, particularly in fields as dynamic and demanding as holographic technology, the pursuit of ambition can often come at the expense of personal well-being. For Kai Ba, the journey was marked by a delicate interplay between striving for groundbreaking achievements and maintaining a healthy, fulfilling life.

Theoretical Background

The concept of work-life balance has been extensively studied in organizational psychology. According to Greenhaus and Allen (2011), work-life balance is defined as the extent to which an individual can meet the demands of both their work and personal life. This balance is crucial for overall well-being, which can be assessed through various dimensions, including psychological, physical, and social health.

$$\text{Well-being} = f(\text{Psychological Health, Physical Health, Social Health}) \quad (45)$$

The equation suggests that well-being is a function of multiple health dimensions, emphasizing the need for a holistic approach to personal development.

Challenges Faced by Kai Ba

Kai Ba's ambition often led him to work long hours, sacrificing sleep and leisure time. This relentless pursuit of success resulted in several challenges:

- **Burnout:** Research indicates that high levels of ambition can lead to burnout, characterized by emotional exhaustion and reduced performance (Maslach et al., 2001). Kai experienced symptoms of burnout, which manifested as chronic fatigue and a sense of disillusionment with his work.

- **Physical Health Issues:** The stress of constant deadlines and high expectations took a toll on Kai's physical health. Studies have shown that prolonged stress can lead to cardiovascular issues, weakened immune response, and other health complications (Kabat-Zinn, 1990).

- **Strained Relationships:** Kai's dedication to his work often resulted in neglecting personal relationships. The social support theory posits that strong social networks contribute positively to well-being (Cohen & Wills, 1985). As Kai became more absorbed in his projects, he found himself increasingly isolated from friends and family.

Strategies for Balancing Ambition and Well-being

To navigate the challenges associated with his ambitious pursuits, Kai Ba adopted several strategies aimed at fostering a healthier balance between work and personal life:

- **Setting Boundaries:** Kai learned the importance of establishing clear boundaries between work and personal time. By designating specific hours for work and leisure, he created a structured schedule that allowed him to recharge and engage in activities outside of his professional commitments.

- **Mindfulness Practices:** Incorporating mindfulness techniques, such as meditation and deep-breathing exercises, helped Kai manage stress levels. Research by Kabat-Zinn (1990) has shown that mindfulness can significantly reduce stress and enhance emotional regulation, leading to improved well-being.

- **Regular Physical Activity:** Understanding the connection between physical health and mental well-being, Kai made a conscious effort to integrate regular exercise into his routine. Physical activity has been linked to the release of endorphins, which can enhance mood and alleviate symptoms of anxiety and depression (Biddle & Asare, 2011).

- **Seeking Support:** Kai recognized the value of social support and began reaching out to friends, family, and colleagues. Engaging in open conversations about his challenges fostered a sense of community and provided him with the emotional resources needed to cope with stress.

Examples of Success and Growth

By implementing these strategies, Kai Ba experienced significant improvements in both his professional output and personal satisfaction. For instance:

- **Increased Productivity:** With a balanced approach to work, Kai found that he could concentrate better and produce higher-quality work. Research supports this notion, indicating that individuals who maintain a healthy work-life balance tend to be more productive and engaged (Kahn & Byosiere, 1992).

- **Enhanced Creativity:** Allowing time for leisure and creativity outside of work led to innovative ideas and solutions for his holographic projects. Studies have shown that diverse experiences and downtime can enhance creative thinking (Finke et al., 1992).

- **Improved Relationships:** By prioritizing relationships, Kai rebuilt connections with friends and family, which contributed to a more fulfilling personal life. The positive effects of social relationships on mental health are well-documented, highlighting the importance of nurturing these bonds (Holt-Lunstad et al., 2010).

Conclusion

In conclusion, the journey of Kai Ba illustrates the critical importance of balancing ambition with well-being. By adopting strategies that promote a healthy lifestyle, he not only enhanced his personal happiness but also improved his professional efficacy. The lessons learned from his experiences serve as a valuable reminder for future innovators: true success lies not just in achievements, but also in the ability to cultivate a life that is rich in both purpose and well-being.

Bibliography

[1] Greenhaus, J. H., & Allen, T. D. (2011). *Work-family balance: A review and extension of the literature*. In J. C. Quick & L. E. Tetrick (Eds.), *Handbook of occupational health psychology* (pp. 165-183). American Psychological Association.

[2] Maslach, C., Schaufeli, W. B., & Leiter, M. P. (2001). *Job burnout*. Annual Review of Psychology, 52(1), 397-422.

[3] Kabat-Zinn, J. (1990). *Full Catastrophe Living: Using the Wisdom of Your Body and Mind to Face Stress, Pain, and Illness*. Delacorte Press.

[4] Biddle, S. J. H., & Asare, M. (2011). *Physical activity and mental health in children and adolescents: A review of reviews*. British Journal of Sports Medicine, 45(11), 886-895.

[5] Finke, R. A., Ward, T. B., & Smith, S. M. (1992). *Creative Cognition: Theory, Research, and Applications*. The MIT Press.

[6] Holt-Lunstad, J., Smith, T. B., & Layton, J. B. (2010). *Social relationships and mortality risk: A meta-analytic review*. PLoS Medicine, 7(7), e1000316.

[7] Kahn, R. L., & Byosiere, P. (1992). *Stress in organizations*. In M. D. Dunnette & L. M. Hough (Eds.), *Handbook of industrial and organizational psychology* (pp. 571-650). Consulting Psychologists Press.

Kai Ba's Stand on Ethical Responsibility

In the rapidly evolving landscape of technology, particularly in the realm of immersive environments, ethical responsibility becomes a paramount concern. Kai Ba, as a pioneer in holographic technology, recognized that the power to create and manipulate virtual realities carries significant ethical implications. His philosophy centered on three core principles: transparency, inclusivity, and accountability.

Transparency in Technology

Kai Ba believed that transparency is crucial in establishing trust between technology developers and users. He advocated for open-source methodologies and encouraged his team to share their findings and innovations with the broader community. This approach aligns with the principles of *open innovation*, which suggests that ideas can come from both internal and external sources, fostering collaboration and collective problem-solving.

To illustrate this, Ba often referenced the development of the Holographic Worlds platform. Early on, he implemented a feedback mechanism allowing users to report issues and suggest improvements. This not only enhanced user experience but also created a culture of continuous improvement. Ba argued that transparency in technology leads to better products and services, as users feel valued and heard.

Inclusivity in Design

Inclusivity was another cornerstone of Ba's ethical framework. He understood that technology should serve diverse populations and that immersive environments must be accessible to all, regardless of socioeconomic status, physical ability, or cultural background. To achieve this, Ba championed the concept of *universal design*, which involves creating products that are usable by everyone.

For example, during the development of the Holographic Worlds platform, Ba insisted on incorporating features such as voice commands, customizable interfaces, and multi-language support. This decision was informed by the principle of *design justice*, which posits that marginalized communities should have a voice in the design process. By prioritizing inclusivity, Ba aimed to create a technology that not only entertained but also empowered users.

Accountability in Innovation

Kai Ba's commitment to accountability was evident in his approach to the ethical implications of virtual reality. He believed that developers must acknowledge the potential consequences of their creations, particularly concerning user behavior and societal impact. This perspective is grounded in *ethical technology*, which asserts that technologists have a responsibility to consider how their products affect individuals and communities.

Ba frequently cited the issue of addiction in virtual environments. He argued that while immersive experiences can provide escapism and entertainment, they can also lead to negative consequences, such as social isolation and dependency. To address this, Ba implemented built-in reminders for users to take breaks and encouraged healthy usage patterns. His stance was that accountability extends beyond the development phase; it requires ongoing monitoring and adaptation to ensure that technology serves the public good.

Case Studies and Theoretical Frameworks

Ba's ethical framework can be further understood through various theoretical lenses. For instance, the *Utilitarianism* theory posits that actions should be evaluated based on their consequences, aiming for the greatest good for the greatest number. Ba applied this principle by weighing the benefits of immersive experiences against potential harms, striving to maximize positive outcomes for users.

Moreover, Ba's approach resonates with *Virtue Ethics*, which emphasizes the character of the moral agent rather than the consequences of specific actions. By fostering a culture of ethical awareness within his team, Ba aimed to cultivate virtuous developers who prioritize the well-being of users.

Conclusion

In conclusion, Kai Ba's stand on ethical responsibility was a multifaceted approach that emphasized transparency, inclusivity, and accountability. By advocating for these principles, he aimed to create a technology landscape that not only innovated but also respected and uplifted the diverse communities it served. As immersive environments continue to evolve, Ba's ethical framework serves as a guiding light for future innovators, reminding them of their profound responsibility to society.

$$E = \frac{U}{R} \tag{46}$$

Where E represents ethical impact, U is the user benefit, and R denotes the risk associated with the technology. This equation encapsulates Ba's philosophy that ethical responsibility can be quantified and should be a fundamental aspect of technological development.

Legacy Beyond Technology

In the exploration of Kai Ba's legacy, it is imperative to recognize that the impact of his work transcends mere technological advancements. While the development of holographic environments and immersive technologies is groundbreaking, the true essence of his legacy lies in the profound societal, cultural, and philosophical changes that these innovations have inspired. This section delves into the multifaceted legacy of Kai Ba, emphasizing the importance of human values, creativity, and ethical considerations in shaping a future that harmonizes technology with the human experience.

Human-Centric Design Philosophy

At the core of Kai Ba's innovations was a commitment to human-centric design. This philosophy posits that technology should serve humanity, enhancing the quality of life rather than detracting from it. Ba believed that immersive environments should not only provide entertainment or efficiency but should also foster connection, empathy, and understanding among users.

An example of this philosophy in action is the development of *Empathy Spaces*, a holographic platform designed to allow users to experience life from the perspective of others, including marginalized communities. By creating scenarios that simulate the challenges faced by individuals from diverse backgrounds, these environments encourage users to develop a deeper understanding of social issues, ultimately promoting compassion and solidarity.

Interdisciplinary Collaboration

Kai Ba's legacy also includes a significant emphasis on interdisciplinary collaboration. He recognized that the most innovative solutions often arise at the intersection of various fields, including art, psychology, sociology, and technology. By fostering partnerships with artists, educators, and social scientists, Ba's Immersive Environments Lab became a crucible for creativity and innovation.

One notable project was the *Cultural Exchange Program*, which brought together technologists and artists from different cultural backgrounds to co-create immersive experiences that highlighted their unique traditions and stories. This initiative not only enriched the technological landscape but also promoted cultural appreciation and dialogue, reinforcing the idea that technology can be a powerful medium for storytelling and cultural preservation.

Ethical Considerations and Social Responsibility

With great power comes great responsibility. As Kai Ba's holographic technologies began to reshape industries and everyday life, he advocated for ethical considerations to be at the forefront of technological development. He emphasized the need for transparency, accountability, and inclusivity in the design and implementation of immersive environments.

Ba's commitment to ethical technology is exemplified by his involvement in the creation of the *Holographic Ethics Board*, a multidisciplinary panel tasked with evaluating the societal implications of new technologies. This board established guidelines to ensure that holographic applications respect user privacy, promote accessibility, and mitigate the risks of addiction and escapism. By prioritizing ethical considerations, Ba set a precedent for future innovators, encouraging them to think critically about the societal impact of their work.

Inspiration for Future Generations

The most enduring aspect of Kai Ba's legacy is his ability to inspire future generations of innovators. By sharing his journey, challenges, and triumphs, he motivated countless individuals to pursue their passions in technology, art, and social justice.

Through mentorship programs and public speaking engagements, Ba encouraged young innovators to think beyond technology and consider the broader implications of their work. His message was clear: innovation is not just about creating new tools; it is about using those tools to create a better world.

One notable initiative, the *Innovators of Tomorrow Summit*, brought together aspiring technologists, artists, and activists to collaborate on projects that addressed pressing social issues. This platform not only nurtured creativity but also instilled a sense of purpose among participants, reinforcing the idea that technology can be a catalyst for positive change.

Philosophical Reflections on Humanity and Technology

Kai Ba's legacy extends into the realm of philosophical inquiry, prompting critical questions about the relationship between humanity and technology. As immersive environments become increasingly integrated into daily life, Ba urged society to reflect on what it means to be human in a digital age.

He often quoted the philosopher Marshall McLuhan, who famously stated, "The medium is the message." Ba believed that as we embrace new technologies, we must remain vigilant about their influence on our values, relationships, and identities. He encouraged ongoing discourse about the implications of living in a world where virtual experiences can sometimes overshadow real-life interactions.

Conclusion

In conclusion, Kai Ba's legacy is not solely defined by his technological innovations but by the profound humanistic principles that underlie his work. His commitment to human-centric design, interdisciplinary collaboration, ethical considerations, and the inspiration of future generations has created a framework for responsible innovation that transcends technology. As we navigate the complexities of an increasingly immersive world, Ba's vision serves as a guiding light, reminding us that the true measure of progress lies in our ability to enhance the human experience while fostering empathy, understanding, and social responsibility.

$$\text{Legacy} = \text{Innovation} + \text{Human Values} + \text{Ethical Responsibility} \tag{47}$$

Reflections on Kai Ba's Journey

Kai Ba's journey is a testament to the transformative power of innovation, creativity, and resilience. Throughout his career, he has encountered numerous challenges that have shaped his character and vision for the future of technology. In this reflection, we explore the key moments and lessons learned from his experiences, emphasizing the importance of adaptability, ethical responsibility, and the pursuit of knowledge.

The Importance of Adaptability

One of the most significant lessons from Kai Ba's journey is the necessity of adaptability in the face of change. As technology evolves at an unprecedented pace, innovators must be willing to pivot their strategies and embrace new paradigms. For instance, during the early development of the Holographic Worlds platform, Kai faced unexpected setbacks due to rapid advancements in artificial intelligence and user interface design. Instead of clinging to his original vision, he recognized the need to incorporate these innovations, which ultimately led to a more robust and user-friendly platform.

This adaptability is encapsulated in the following equation, which represents the relationship between adaptability (A), external change (C), and innovation success (I):

$$I = A \cdot C \tag{48}$$

Where: - I is the measure of innovation success, - A is the level of adaptability, - C is the magnitude of external change.

Kai's ability to adapt not only enhanced the platform's functionality but also fostered a culture of innovation within his team, encouraging them to embrace change as an opportunity rather than a threat.

Ethical Responsibility in Innovation

As Kai Ba ventured deeper into the realm of immersive environments, he became acutely aware of the ethical implications of his work. The power of holographic technology to influence perceptions and behaviors raises critical questions about responsibility. Kai firmly believed that with great power comes great responsibility, echoing the sentiments of renowned ethicist Peter Singer, who argues for the moral obligation of innovators to consider the broader impact of their creations.

For instance, as the Holographic Worlds platform began to gain traction in various sectors, including healthcare and education, Kai initiated discussions on ethical guidelines for the use of immersive technology. This proactive approach is summarized in the following ethical framework:

$$E = R + S + C \tag{49}$$

Where: - E represents ethical responsibility, - R is the respect for user autonomy, - S is the commitment to social justice, - C is the consideration of cultural sensitivity.

By integrating these elements into the development process, Kai ensured that the technology would be used to empower individuals and communities rather than exploit them.

The Pursuit of Knowledge

Kai Ba's insatiable curiosity and commitment to lifelong learning have been instrumental in his success. He often reflects on the early days of his career when he sought mentorship from seasoned professionals in the field. This mentorship not only provided him with valuable insights but also instilled in him the importance of continuous education.

In his journey, Kai adopted a growth mindset, as described by psychologist Carol Dweck, which emphasizes the belief that abilities can be developed through dedication and hard work. This mindset is critical in fostering resilience and a love for learning, leading to greater innovation.

The equation representing the relationship between knowledge acquisition (K), effort (E), and innovation potential (P) can be expressed as follows:

$$P = K \cdot E \tag{50}$$

Where: - P is the innovation potential, - K is the level of knowledge acquired, - E is the effort put into learning.

Kai's commitment to expanding his knowledge base allowed him to stay ahead of industry trends and inspire his team to pursue their intellectual curiosities.

Building a Supportive Community

Throughout his career, Kai has emphasized the importance of building a supportive community of innovators. He often reflects on the early days of establishing the Immersive Environments Lab, where he focused on creating an inclusive and collaborative environment. This community not only fostered creativity but also provided emotional and professional support during challenging times.

Research has shown that collaborative environments can significantly enhance innovation outcomes. The following equation illustrates the relationship between community support (C) and innovation output (O):

$$O = C^2 \qquad (51)$$

Where: - O is the innovation output, - C is the level of community support.

By nurturing a culture of collaboration, Kai enabled his team to share ideas freely, leading to groundbreaking advancements in holographic technology.

Legacy and Future Aspirations

As Kai Ba reflects on his journey, he recognizes the profound impact of his work on future generations. He is committed to inspiring young innovators and advocates for education that emphasizes creativity, critical thinking, and ethical responsibility. His vision for the future includes a world where technology serves humanity, bridging gaps and fostering understanding across cultures.

In conclusion, Kai Ba's journey is a rich tapestry of challenges, lessons, and triumphs. His adaptability, commitment to ethical responsibility, pursuit of knowledge, and dedication to building a supportive community have shaped not only his career but also the future of holographic technology. As he continues to innovate, his legacy will undoubtedly inspire future generations to embrace the transformative power of creativity and technology.

Epilogue: The Future of Holographic Worlds

The Evolution of Immersive Environments

Current Trends and Innovations

In the rapidly evolving landscape of immersive environments, several current trends and innovations are shaping the way holographic worlds are developed and integrated into various sectors. These trends not only reflect technological advancements but also the shifting paradigms in user interaction, accessibility, and ethical considerations. This section delves into the most significant trends influencing the future of holographic worlds.

Enhanced User Interfaces

One of the most prominent trends in holographic technology is the development of enhanced user interfaces (UIs) that prioritize user experience. Traditional input methods, such as keyboards and mice, are being replaced by more intuitive systems that leverage gesture recognition, voice commands, and even brain-computer interfaces (BCIs). For example, companies like *Magic Leap* and *Microsoft* are pioneering mixed-reality headsets that allow users to interact with holograms using natural hand movements and spoken commands.

The theoretical underpinning of these advancements can be traced back to *Human-Computer Interaction (HCI)* principles, which emphasize the need for systems that are not only functional but also user-friendly. As noted by Shneiderman (2020), effective UIs should be designed to minimize user effort while maximizing engagement and satisfaction.

Artificial Intelligence Integration

Artificial intelligence (AI) is increasingly being integrated into holographic environments to create more dynamic and responsive experiences. AI algorithms can analyze user behavior in real time, adapting the holographic content to suit individual preferences and needs. For instance, *NVIDIA* has developed AI-driven tools that enhance the realism of holographic imagery by predicting and rendering high-quality graphics based on user interactions.

The mathematical models behind these AI systems often involve deep learning techniques, particularly convolutional neural networks (CNNs), which excel at processing visual data. The performance of a CNN can be represented by the equation:

$$y = f(W \cdot x + b) \tag{52}$$

where y is the output, W represents the weights of the network, x is the input data, and b is the bias. This equation highlights how AI can learn and adapt based on the data it processes, leading to more immersive and personalized holographic experiences.

Cross-Platform Compatibility

As the demand for immersive experiences grows, there is a notable trend towards cross-platform compatibility. Developers are increasingly focused on creating holographic applications that can function seamlessly across various devices, including smartphones, tablets, and dedicated VR/AR headsets. This approach not only broadens the accessibility of holographic worlds but also encourages collaborative experiences among users on different platforms.

A pertinent example is the use of web-based technologies such as *WebXR*, which allows developers to create immersive experiences that can be accessed directly through web browsers. This trend aligns with the principles of *ubiquitous computing*, which advocate for technology that is integrated into everyday life, making it more accessible and less obtrusive.

Focus on Accessibility and Inclusivity

The importance of accessibility in technology is gaining recognition, and this is reflected in the design of holographic environments. Developers are now prioritizing inclusivity, ensuring that holographic experiences are accessible to individuals with disabilities. Innovations such as customizable interfaces, audio descriptions, and adaptive controls are being implemented to cater to a diverse audience.

The theoretical framework for this trend is grounded in the *Universal Design* principles, which advocate for designing products that are usable by all people, to the greatest extent possible. Research by Mace (1985) emphasizes that universal design not only benefits individuals with disabilities but also enhances the overall user experience for everyone.

Ethical Considerations in Holographic Worlds

As holographic technologies become more pervasive, ethical considerations surrounding their use are increasingly coming to the forefront. Issues related to privacy, data security, and the potential for addiction are significant concerns that developers must address. For example, the integration of biometric data in user interfaces raises questions about how this information is stored and utilized.

The ethical framework for these considerations can be analyzed through the lens of *Utilitarianism*, which posits that actions should be evaluated based on their consequences. Developers are encouraged to adopt ethical guidelines that prioritize user safety and well-being, ensuring that the benefits of holographic technologies outweigh the potential risks.

Environmental Sustainability

Another emerging trend is the focus on environmental sustainability within the realm of holographic technologies. As concerns about climate change and resource depletion grow, developers are exploring ways to reduce the environmental impact of their products. This includes optimizing energy consumption in holographic devices and utilizing sustainable materials in hardware production.

The theoretical basis for this trend is rooted in the principles of *Sustainable Development*, which advocate for meeting the needs of the present without compromising the ability of future generations to meet their own needs. By prioritizing sustainability, the holographic industry can contribute to a more responsible and eco-friendly technological landscape.

Conclusion

In conclusion, the current trends and innovations in holographic worlds reflect a dynamic intersection of technology, user experience, and ethical considerations. Enhanced user interfaces, AI integration, cross-platform compatibility, accessibility, ethical frameworks, and sustainability are all critical components shaping the future of immersive environments. As these trends continue to evolve, they will pave the way for more engaging, responsible, and inclusive holographic experiences that resonate with a diverse global audience.

Potential Challenges and Solutions

The evolution of holographic worlds presents a myriad of challenges that must be addressed to ensure the technology's sustainable and ethical growth. This section explores these challenges, categorizing them into technical, ethical, and societal dimensions, while proposing potential solutions to mitigate their impacts.

Technical Challenges

1. **Hardware Limitations**   One of the foremost challenges in developing immersive holographic environments is the limitation of current hardware. High-quality holography requires advanced display technologies that can render three-dimensional images with precision. Current devices often struggle with resolution and refresh rates, leading to a less immersive experience.

$$\text{Resolution} = \frac{\text{Pixel Count}}{\text{Field of View}} \times \text{Distance} \qquad (53)$$

To overcome these limitations, research into new materials, such as meta-materials and liquid crystal displays (LCDs), is essential. Innovations like microLED technology can provide higher resolutions and better color accuracy, paving the way for more immersive experiences.

2. **Software Integration**   As holographic technology advances, the need for robust software solutions becomes paramount. Current software frameworks often lack the capability to seamlessly integrate various aspects of holographic environments, such as user interactions and real-time rendering.

A potential solution lies in developing unified software platforms that can handle multiple data streams and user inputs efficiently. Utilizing cloud computing and edge computing can also distribute processing loads, enhancing performance.

Ethical Challenges

1. **Privacy Concerns**   With the rise of immersive environments, the collection and utilization of personal data pose significant ethical dilemmas. Users' interactions within these spaces can generate vast amounts of data, raising concerns about privacy and consent.

To address these issues, companies must implement transparent data policies that inform users about data collection practices. Employing encryption techniques and decentralized data storage can enhance security and give users more control over their information.

2. Digital Divide The accessibility of holographic technology remains a critical challenge. There is a risk that these advancements may widen the gap between those with access to technology and those without, exacerbating existing inequalities.

To combat this, initiatives should focus on making holographic technology more affordable and accessible. Government subsidies and partnerships with educational institutions can facilitate access in underprivileged communities, ensuring equitable distribution of technology.

Societal Challenges

1. Addiction and Escapism As holographic worlds become increasingly immersive, the potential for addiction and escapism grows. Users may find themselves preferring virtual experiences over real-life interactions, leading to social isolation and mental health issues.

To mitigate these risks, developers should incorporate features that promote healthy usage patterns. Implementing time limits, reminders, and encouraging real-world interactions can help users maintain a balanced relationship with technology.

2. Employment Displacement The automation of tasks through holographic technologies may lead to job displacement in various sectors. As industries adopt these innovations, workers may find their roles obsolete, creating economic challenges.

A proactive approach is essential to address this concern. Upskilling and reskilling programs can prepare the workforce for new roles that emerge alongside holographic technologies. Collaboration between governments, educational institutions, and industries can facilitate transitions into new job markets.

Conclusion

The potential challenges associated with the evolution of holographic worlds are multifaceted, spanning technical, ethical, and societal domains. By identifying these challenges and proposing viable solutions, stakeholders can work collaboratively to navigate the complexities of this transformative technology.

Ensuring that holographic environments are developed responsibly and inclusively will be crucial in shaping a future where innovation benefits all members of society.

Holographic Worlds v2.0

As we venture into the next iteration of holographic technology, dubbed Holographic Worlds v2.0, we find ourselves at the intersection of advanced computational power, immersive experiences, and ethical considerations. This evolution is not merely about enhancing visual fidelity or interactivity; it encapsulates a paradigm shift in how we perceive and engage with digital environments.

Theoretical Foundations

Holographic Worlds v2.0 is built on several theoretical frameworks that guide its development. One of the primary theories is the *Immersive Experience Theory*, which posits that deeper engagement with virtual environments can lead to enhanced learning, empathy, and creativity. This theory is supported by research indicating that immersive experiences can significantly improve retention rates in educational settings, as noted by Smith et al. (2021). The equation governing user engagement can be expressed as:

$$E = \frac{I \times R}{D} \tag{54}$$

where E is engagement, I represents interactivity, R is realism, and D is distraction. This equation underscores the importance of balancing these elements to foster an engaging experience.

Technological Advancements

At the core of Holographic Worlds v2.0 are advancements in several key technologies:

- **Artificial Intelligence (AI):** The integration of AI allows for dynamic content generation, enabling environments that adapt to user behaviors and preferences in real-time. For instance, AI algorithms can analyze user interactions to tailor experiences, enhancing personalization.

- **Edge Computing:** By processing data closer to the source, edge computing reduces latency, resulting in smoother and more responsive holographic

THE EVOLUTION OF IMMERSIVE ENVIRONMENTS

experiences. This is crucial in applications such as remote surgery or collaborative design, where real-time feedback is essential.

- **Neural Interfaces:** Emerging neural interface technologies offer direct communication between the human brain and holographic systems, enabling users to manipulate virtual environments through thought alone. This concept, while still in its infancy, opens up unprecedented possibilities for accessibility and control.

Problems and Challenges

Despite these advancements, several challenges persist in the development of Holographic Worlds v2.0:

- **Data Privacy and Security:** With increased interactivity comes the risk of data breaches. As users engage more deeply with holographic systems, the amount of personal data generated skyrockets. Ensuring that this data is protected is paramount. The equation for data vulnerability can be represented as:

$$V = \frac{P \times E}{C} \qquad (55)$$

where V is vulnerability, P is the amount of personal data, E is exposure level, and C is the complexity of security measures.

- **Digital Divide:** As holographic technology becomes more sophisticated, the risk of exacerbating existing inequalities increases. Access to the necessary hardware and internet bandwidth is not universal, potentially leaving marginalized communities behind.

- **User Overload:** With the richness of immersive environments, users may experience cognitive overload, leading to diminished returns in engagement and learning. Finding the right balance in complexity and simplicity is crucial.

Examples of Holographic Worlds v2.0 in Action

Several pioneering projects exemplify the potential of Holographic Worlds v2.0:

- **HoloMed:** A healthcare application that utilizes holographic simulations for medical training. Trainees can interact with 3D holograms of human anatomy, allowing for a deeper understanding of complex structures and procedures.

- **EduHolo:** An educational platform that creates immersive learning environments for students. By simulating historical events or scientific phenomena, students can engage with content in a way that traditional methods cannot replicate.

- **HoloSport:** A mixed-reality sports training program that combines holographic feedback with real-world practice. Athletes can visualize their performance metrics in real-time, allowing for immediate adjustments and improvements.

Conclusion

Holographic Worlds v2.0 represents not just a technological evolution but a fundamental shift in how we interact with digital realities. As we navigate this new landscape, it is imperative to address the ethical implications, ensuring that these innovations serve to enhance human experiences rather than detract from them. The future of immersive environments holds the promise of transforming industries, education, and personal interactions, paving the way for a more interconnected and enriched world.

The Ever-Expanding Universe of Imagination

The concept of the "Ever-Expanding Universe of Imagination" encapsulates the limitless potential of holographic worlds and their capacity to transform not only our interactions with technology but also our very understanding of creativity and innovation. As we delve into this expansive realm, we must consider the theoretical frameworks, challenges, and applications that shape our engagement with these immersive environments.

Theoretical Frameworks

At the heart of the holographic experience lies the interplay between perception, cognition, and creativity. Theories such as *Constructivist Learning Theory* suggest that knowledge is constructed through interaction with the environment, which in the case of holographic worlds, is enhanced through immersive experiences. According to Piaget's stages of cognitive development, individuals move from concrete operational stages to more abstract thinking as they engage with complex environments. Holographic worlds facilitate this transition by enabling users to manipulate and explore three-dimensional spaces, thereby fostering deeper learning and creativity.

Moreover, the *Flow Theory*, proposed by Mihaly Csikszentmihalyi, emphasizes the state of flow that individuals experience when fully immersed in an activity. Holographic environments are designed to induce this state by providing optimal challenges that match the user's skill level, thus promoting creativity and innovation. The equation that encapsulates this experience can be expressed as:

$$\text{Flow} = \text{Challenge Level} - \text{Skill Level} \qquad (56)$$

When the challenge level exceeds skill level, individuals may experience anxiety, while a challenge level that is too low can lead to boredom. The ideal state of flow occurs when challenge and skill are balanced, allowing for the maximum creative output.

Challenges in Imagination Expansion

Despite the promising potential of holographic worlds, several challenges must be addressed to fully harness their imaginative capabilities. One significant issue is the *digital divide*, which refers to the disparities in access to technology among different socioeconomic groups. This divide hinders equal participation in the imaginative opportunities offered by holographic environments. For instance, individuals from underprivileged backgrounds may lack access to the necessary hardware or software, thus limiting their ability to engage with these transformative technologies.

Additionally, the *ethics of imagination* must be considered. As we create more realistic and immersive environments, questions arise regarding the implications of virtual experiences on real-world behavior. The potential for desensitization to violence, the blurring of reality and fiction, and the influence of virtual experiences on moral decision-making are pressing concerns. It is crucial to establish ethical guidelines that govern the creation and use of holographic content to ensure that imagination is expanded positively and constructively.

Examples of Imagination in Holographic Worlds

The practical applications of holographic worlds provide a glimpse into their imaginative potential. For example, in the field of education, institutions are utilizing holographic simulations to teach complex subjects such as biology and physics. Students can interact with three-dimensional models of cells or physical phenomena, allowing for a more engaging and effective learning experience. A notable case is the use of holography in medical training, where students can practice surgical procedures in a risk-free environment, enhancing their skills and confidence before operating on real patients.

In the realm of art and entertainment, holographic performances have revolutionized live shows. Artists like Tupac Shakur have been brought back to life through holographic projections, allowing fans to experience concerts in a way that was previously unimaginable. This not only expands the boundaries of artistic expression but also raises questions about the implications of resurrecting figures from the past.

Furthermore, the gaming industry has embraced holographic technology, with developers creating immersive experiences that allow players to step into fantastical worlds. Games that utilize augmented reality, such as *Pokémon GO*, encourage players to explore their physical environments while interacting with digital creatures, effectively blending the boundaries between reality and imagination.

The Future of Imagination in Holographic Worlds

Looking ahead, the potential for the ever-expanding universe of imagination within holographic worlds is boundless. As technology advances, we can anticipate the emergence of more sophisticated holographic interfaces that will further enhance user engagement and creativity. The integration of artificial intelligence will personalize experiences, adapting to individual preferences and learning styles, thereby fostering a more profound connection between users and their virtual environments.

Moreover, as we explore the implications of virtual reality for social interaction, we may witness the development of virtual communities that transcend geographical boundaries. These communities could facilitate collaboration and creativity on a global scale, allowing individuals from diverse backgrounds to share ideas and innovate together.

In conclusion, the ever-expanding universe of imagination within holographic worlds represents a frontier of creativity and innovation. By addressing the challenges of access and ethics, and by harnessing the theoretical frameworks that underpin human cognition and creativity, we can unlock the full potential of these immersive environments. The future promises a rich tapestry of experiences that will redefine our understanding of imagination, creativity, and human connection in ways we are only beginning to comprehend.

The Legacy of Holographic Worlds

The legacy of holographic worlds is not merely a testament to technological advancement but also a reflection of the profound impact these innovations have had on society, culture, and the human experience. As we delve into the various dimensions of this legacy, it is essential to consider both the theoretical frameworks that underpin holographic technologies and the practical implications they have engendered.

Theoretical Foundations

At its core, the concept of holographic worlds is rooted in the principles of holography, which employs the interference of light waves to create three-dimensional images. This technology has evolved significantly since its inception, with applications extending beyond mere visualization to encompass immersive experiences that engage multiple senses. The theories of perception, presence, and embodiment play crucial roles in understanding the impact of holographic environments.

Presence Theory Presence theory posits that individuals experience a sense of "being there" in a virtual environment, which can significantly alter their perception and interaction with that space. This phenomenon is underpinned by the following equation:

$$P = f(S, I, E) \qquad (57)$$

where P represents the sense of presence, S denotes sensory input, I signifies the interactivity of the environment, and E encapsulates the emotional engagement of the user. This equation suggests that a higher degree of sensory input, interactivity, and emotional connection leads to a stronger sense of presence, thereby enhancing the overall experience within holographic worlds.

Societal Impacts

The integration of holographic worlds into various sectors has led to transformative changes in how we interact with information, each other, and our environment. The implications of these changes are broad and multifaceted.

Healthcare Revolution In healthcare, holographic technologies have enabled groundbreaking advancements in surgical procedures and patient education. For instance, surgeons can now visualize complex anatomical structures in three dimensions, leading to improved precision during operations. A notable example is the use of holographic imaging in neurosurgery, where practitioners can overlay digital models of the brain onto a patient's actual anatomy, enhancing the accuracy of interventions.

Education and Training Holographic worlds have also revolutionized education and training. By creating immersive learning environments, educators can facilitate experiential learning that transcends traditional classroom boundaries. For example, medical students can practice surgical techniques in a risk-free holographic environment, allowing for repeated practice and mastery before engaging with real patients.

Cultural Shifts

The cultural legacy of holographic worlds is equally significant. As these technologies become more integrated into daily life, they reshape our interactions and relationships. The concept of shared experiences in virtual spaces has given rise to new forms of social interaction, where individuals can connect regardless of geographical barriers.

Virtual Communities The emergence of virtual communities, facilitated by holographic platforms, has fostered a sense of belonging among users who share common interests. These communities often engage in collaborative projects, ranging from art to activism, demonstrating the potential of holographic worlds to unite individuals around shared goals.

Ethical Considerations

As with any technological advancement, the legacy of holographic worlds is accompanied by ethical considerations that must be addressed. The potential for misuse of these technologies raises questions about privacy, consent, and the blurring of lines between reality and virtuality.

Privacy and Data Security The collection of data within holographic environments necessitates robust security measures to protect user information. Ethical frameworks must be established to ensure that users are informed about data usage and that their privacy is respected. The equation governing ethical data use can be expressed as:

$$E = \frac{D}{C} \tag{58}$$

where E represents ethical integrity, D denotes the degree of data transparency, and C signifies the consent of users. A higher value of E indicates a more ethical approach to data management.

Future Directions

Looking ahead, the legacy of holographic worlds will continue to evolve as technology advances. Future innovations may include enhanced sensory experiences through haptic feedback and olfactory elements, further bridging the gap between virtual and real-world interactions. The potential for environmental sustainability through virtualization also presents exciting possibilities, allowing for the reduction of physical resources in various industries.

Sustainability and Virtualization The concept of virtualization as a means of promoting sustainability can be expressed through the equation:

$$S = \frac{R}{E} \tag{59}$$

where S represents sustainability, R denotes the reduction of resource consumption, and E signifies the efficiency of virtual processes. As holographic worlds become more efficient, they will play a crucial role in minimizing our ecological footprint.

In conclusion, the legacy of holographic worlds is a rich tapestry woven from threads of innovation, societal change, and ethical reflection. As we continue to explore the potential of these immersive environments, it is imperative that we remain mindful of their implications, ensuring that they contribute positively to the fabric of human experience. The journey of holographic worlds is just beginning, and their legacy will undoubtedly shape the future of technology and society for generations to come.

Index

-doubt, 16

a, 1–7, 9, 12, 14–17, 20–30, 33, 35–38, 40–53, 55–57, 60–63, 65–70, 73, 74, 76–80, 82, 84–88, 91, 92, 96, 97, 99, 104–107, 109, 111, 113–115, 117, 119–121, 123–127, 129–135, 137, 139–146, 149–152, 154–159
ability, 22, 25, 28, 29, 33, 50, 53, 67, 76, 84, 87, 123, 137, 143, 144
academic, 12, 16, 17, 26, 45, 48–50, 127, 128
acceptance, 25, 51, 134
access, 26, 48, 52, 67, 73, 77, 80, 83, 86, 104–106, 120, 124, 125, 151, 156
accessibility, 29, 56, 66, 77, 109, 119, 121, 147–149, 151
accountability, 139, 141, 142
accuracy, 63, 69, 70
acquisition, 49
activism, 158
adaptability, 46, 53, 144, 146
adaptation, 36, 141

addiction, 79, 99, 103, 104, 134, 140, 149, 151
addition, 2, 125, 128, 131
adoption, 29, 36, 37
advance, 37
advancement, 7, 51, 106, 111, 117, 129, 133, 157, 158
advent, 73, 76, 83, 91, 94, 97, 99, 104, 109, 111
adventure, 88
advocacy, 123–125, 130
advocate, 106, 132
age, 1, 3, 15, 143
agency, 114
aid, 52
allocation, 46, 66
Amartya Sen, 104
ambiguity, 84
ambition, 134, 135, 137
analysis, 78
anatomy, 68, 69
anxiety, 87, 103, 155
application, 15, 57
approach, 5, 15, 17, 24, 26, 40, 42, 45, 47, 50, 60, 73, 83, 86, 88, 113, 115, 117, 123, 124, 130, 135, 141, 145, 151

architecture, 67, 76–78
area, 78
art, 14, 20, 21, 44, 142, 143, 156, 158
artificial, 70, 115, 144, 156
aspect, 143
assembly, 44
assessment, 116
astronomy, 1, 28, 91–94
athlete, 78
atmosphere, 3, 87
audience, 2, 67, 79, 133, 149, 150
audio, 148
auditory, 84
authentication, 67
authenticity, 18, 29, 115
automation, 151
autonomy, 26
availability, 47
awareness, 99, 102, 125

Ba, 124, 125, 140–142, 144
background, 3
backing, 47
backup, 84
balance, 38, 44, 45, 50, 113, 133, 135
barrier, 37
base, 146
basketball, 78, 79
baton, 119
battle, 23
beacon, 119, 130
beauty, 14
bedrock, 20
behavior, 21, 39
being, 40, 57, 87, 104, 107, 117, 134, 135, 137, 149
Belbin, 44
belief, 16, 41, 53, 123, 145

belonging, 158
benchmark, 62
benefit, 105, 109
bias, 62
biology, 1, 19, 155
birth, 79
birthday, 1
blend, 33, 65
blueprint, 50
body, 117
boredom, 155
breeding, 131
building, 77, 96, 146
burnout, 133

camaraderie, 45
camp, 16
campaign, 24
canvas, 5
capability, 36, 69, 105, 150
capacity, 154
capturing, 50, 65
care, 19, 80
career, 25, 119, 120, 127, 129, 132, 144–146
Carol Dweck, 53, 145
case, 20, 34, 75, 101, 106, 130, 156
catalyst, 5
challenge, 24, 26, 29, 47, 56, 65–67, 87, 91, 115, 124, 125, 151, 155
change, 16, 27, 37, 60, 144, 149, 159
character, 132, 144
charge, 43
Chen, 26
child, 15
childhood, 1, 2
clarity, 63
classroom, 36, 124, 158

climate, 149
cloud, 150
club, 2
co, 27, 126
coding, 15, 16
cognition, 66, 156
coherence, 29
cohesion, 46
collaboration, 2, 4, 21–24, 27, 35, 41, 43, 46, 69, 76, 78, 83–86, 90, 91, 94, 109–111, 113, 117, 124, 130, 132, 142, 144, 146, 156
collection, 39, 87, 150, 151, 158
college, 123
colonization, 86, 88
colony, 86, 88
combination, 67
comfort, 88
commitment, 17, 22, 27, 43, 53, 120, 123, 130, 134, 142, 144–146
committee, 24
communication, 24, 26, 44, 46, 83, 84, 86, 124
community, 5, 15–17, 24, 52, 120, 125, 146
companion, 115
companionship, 115
company, 126
compatibility, 67, 149
competence, 22
competition, 44, 78–80
complexity, 23, 24, 27, 29, 65, 77
component, 27, 82, 91, 119
comprehension, 19
computer, 15, 23, 30
computing, 37, 66, 150

concept, 86, 113, 154, 157–159
conception, 105
conceptualization, 35
concern, 69, 105, 139, 151
conclusion, 2, 7, 9, 17, 20, 22, 27, 30, 32, 35, 37, 49, 67, 70, 75, 78, 80, 86, 88, 91, 99, 104, 111, 115, 129, 132, 137, 141, 143, 146, 149, 156, 159
confidence, 4, 22, 55, 156
confirmation, 55
conflict, 46
confluence, 14
confusion, 56, 99
connection, 43, 101, 115, 142, 156
consciousness, 114
consent, 29, 40, 150, 158
conservation, 20
consideration, 39, 66, 67, 77, 88
constant, 23
construct, 42, 115
construction, 77, 85, 88
constructivism, 71
consumption, 77, 149
content, 32, 33, 37, 39, 42, 55, 60
context, 7, 20, 57, 73, 77, 104, 105
contingency, 84
control, 39, 67, 85, 151
cooperation, 105
core, 27, 30, 41, 92, 139, 142, 152, 157
cornerstone, 53, 123
cosmos, 83, 94
course, 124
creation, 27, 57, 60, 68, 107
creativity, 3, 7, 12, 15, 20, 22, 26, 27, 45, 60, 62, 109, 111, 119,

121, 123, 125, 130, 142, 144, 146, 154, 156
credit, 29
crowdfunding, 24
crucible, 142
cultivation, 119, 121
culture, 15, 24, 45, 46, 53, 125, 131, 140, 144, 146, 157
curiosity, 1–3, 14, 15, 17, 130, 145
curricula, 22, 25, 124, 125, 130
curve, 23
cusp, 30
customer, 37
cutting, 26, 48, 52, 119, 125, 130
cycle, 27, 36

data, 23, 39, 62, 66, 67, 79, 80, 83, 86, 87, 92, 94, 96, 134, 149–151, 158
David Chalmers, 114
day, 88
decision, 89
dedication, 53, 125, 145, 146
degradation, 20
degree, 21
demonstration, 50, 51
department, 52
dependency, 26, 87, 140
depletion, 149
depression, 87
depth, 68
design, 2, 9, 21, 23, 27, 36, 37, 56, 57, 65–67, 76–78, 87, 91, 133, 142, 144, 148
desire, 2, 16
detachment, 77
detail, 29, 63
deterrent, 29

development, 5, 20, 21, 24, 27, 33, 40, 48, 50, 52, 65, 67, 89, 106, 117, 124, 130, 131, 135, 140–142, 144, 145, 153, 156
device, 67, 127
dialogue, 14, 65, 106, 125
difference, 105
difficulty, 25
diffraction, 27, 92, 107
diffusion, 127
direction, 46
disappointment, 23
discipline, 20
discourse, 115, 143
discovery, 17
discrepancy, 26
discussion, 130
disengagement, 66
displacement, 151
display, 78, 85, 150
distinction, 97
distraction, 102
distribution, 104, 151
diversity, 14, 60, 125, 131
divide, 52, 79, 97–99, 105, 115
doubt, 16, 53
dream, 7, 44, 46
dust, 87
dynamic, 46, 47, 61, 125, 134, 149

Earth, 84–88, 91
ecosystem, 127
edge, 26, 48, 52, 66, 119, 125, 130, 150
education, 9, 15, 22, 27, 28, 36, 37, 68, 71–73, 83, 109, 123, 125, 126, 130, 145, 146, 154, 155, 158

Index 165

effect, 127
effectiveness, 22, 37, 62, 72
efficacy, 70, 137
efficiency, 77, 89, 109, 111, 142
effort, 99, 132
element, 62
Elena Torres, 4
embodiment, 157
emergence, 21, 156, 158
emergency, 69, 85
Emily Chen, 126
emotion, 53
empathy, 2, 142, 144
emphasis, 142
empowerment, 105, 106, 121, 123
encouragement, 5
encryption, 67, 151
end, 20, 67, 123
endeavor, 16, 43, 60, 65, 115
energy, 77, 149
engagement, 15, 17, 19, 21, 25, 35–37, 52, 57, 60, 73, 74, 76, 78, 80, 83, 94, 102, 104, 127, 154, 156
engineering, 23
enhancement, 62, 78, 114
enjoyment, 79
enrollment, 52
entertainment, 5, 9, 28, 29, 73, 75, 76, 109, 140, 142, 156
entrepreneurship, 132
environment, 3, 12, 15, 22, 24, 42, 45, 46, 51, 56, 57, 61, 63, 74, 85, 87, 107, 126, 133, 146, 156–158
equation, 21, 22, 35, 38, 39, 50, 53, 65, 68, 73, 78, 87, 126, 133, 135, 158, 159
equipment, 29

equity, 77, 104, 115
era, 30, 73, 94, 99, 109
escape, 102
escapism, 103, 104, 140, 151
essence, 33, 69, 80, 114, 141
establishment, 47, 49, 88, 117
estate, 36
ethicist, 145
evolution, 25, 68, 89, 117, 150–152, 154
example, 28, 36, 42, 45, 57, 62, 67, 78–80, 84, 115, 120, 124, 127, 131, 149, 155, 158
exclusion, 105
execution, 84, 86
exercise, 12
exhilaration, 16
existence, 113, 115
expense, 134
experience, 2, 9, 12, 14, 16, 21, 25, 28, 29, 35–37, 40–42, 44, 50, 57, 61, 62, 65, 68, 73, 74, 76–78, 84, 88, 97, 99, 103, 109, 115, 140, 142, 144, 149, 150, 155–157, 159
experiment, 88
experimentation, 35
expertise, 17, 22, 23, 48, 49, 52, 67
exploration, 7, 12, 15, 82, 83, 86, 88, 91, 94, 115, 141
exposure, 3, 14, 26, 119
expression, 156
extent, 39, 63, 74

fabric, 22, 159
face, 4, 17, 84, 144
failure, 17, 26, 53, 133
fairness, 105

family, 1–5, 17
fan, 78, 80
fantasy, 102
fascination, 2
fear, 53
feasibility, 23
feature, 131
feedback, 44, 55, 57, 62, 66, 78, 140, 159
feeling, 43, 84
fiction, 3, 5–7
fidelity, 62, 152
field, 16, 17, 20, 22, 25, 28, 30, 36, 47, 50, 57, 65, 68, 92, 107, 125, 127–129, 134, 145, 155
figure, 2
fit, 45
fitness, 79
flow, 77, 155
focus, 42, 45, 149, 151
footprint, 111
force, 3, 17, 25, 55
forefront, 35, 117, 142, 149
forgery, 29
form, 78, 103
foster, 40, 43, 45, 99, 100, 111, 132, 142
foundation, 3, 17, 46, 50, 57, 117, 133
founder, 27, 53, 130
framework, 30, 66, 117, 141, 144, 145
freedom, 105
Friedland, 27
frontier, 30, 88, 156
frustration, 23, 66
function, 21, 35, 38, 63, 73, 135
functionality, 144
funding, 23, 24, 47, 124, 127
future, 1, 3, 5, 15, 17, 22, 25, 27, 34, 37, 40, 44, 50, 55, 57, 60, 65, 68, 70, 73, 76, 80, 83, 86, 91, 94, 96, 99, 106, 109, 113, 115–117, 119, 121, 125, 127, 130–132, 134, 137, 141–144, 146, 147, 150, 152, 154, 156, 159

gain, 145
game, 79
gameplay, 29, 74
gaming, 29, 73, 75
gap, 105, 151, 159
generation, 5, 27, 119, 123, 125, 130
genre, 7
gesture, 56, 66
gift, 1, 15
glimpse, 155
good, 45, 105, 141
governance, 115, 116
ground, 5, 85, 131
groundbreaking, 4, 5, 17, 20, 27, 50, 55, 68, 119, 128, 130, 133, 134, 141, 146
groundwork, 1, 15, 26, 121
group, 124
grow, 149
growth, 5, 16, 27, 53, 55, 67, 96, 134, 145, 150
guidance, 2, 4, 5, 26, 27, 119, 120

habitat, 85, 88
hand, 57
happiness, 137
haptic, 159
hardware, 30, 37, 67, 84, 149, 150

Index

harness, 41, 91, 102, 106
head, 134
headset, 67
healing, 115
health, 131, 135, 151
healthcare, 9, 27, 28, 57, 62, 68–70, 109, 126, 127, 145
heart, 57
heritage, 18
history, 18, 42, 126
hologram, 107
holography, 17, 20, 27–30, 41, 59, 68, 70, 91, 94, 109, 123, 125, 130, 150, 156, 157
home, 1, 83
honor, 131
household, 15
human, 3, 9, 32, 40, 41, 60, 65, 68, 77, 78, 86–91, 97, 99–102, 104, 113–115, 117, 142–144, 154, 156, 157, 159
humanity, 17, 27, 41, 43, 83, 85, 86, 88, 113, 115, 142, 143, 146
hurdle, 23, 29, 133
hype, 23

idea, 1, 55, 63, 113
ideal, 155
identity, 14, 97, 99, 113–115
illusion, 23
image, 29
imagination, 5, 20, 65, 109, 156
imaging, 28
imitation, 39
immersion, 29, 38, 66, 74, 75, 82
impact, 3, 5, 9, 12, 21, 23, 26, 27, 31, 34, 38, 57, 76–78, 94, 99, 100, 104, 113, 120, 125–129, 141, 145, 146, 149, 157
implementation, 28, 57, 66, 72, 86, 106, 142
importance, 2, 4, 5, 15, 20, 24, 27, 43, 44, 46, 49, 52, 84, 105, 124, 125, 128, 137, 142, 144–146, 148
improvement, 38, 78, 140
inadequacy, 53
inception, 157
inclusion, 125
inclusivity, 12, 40, 73, 106, 125, 132, 134, 139, 141, 142, 148
income, 124
incorporation, 107
individual, 5, 15, 37, 86, 125, 128, 156
industry, 27, 36, 37, 40, 45, 47–51, 80, 119, 124, 125, 128, 146
infancy, 29
influence, 3–5, 91, 121, 127, 129, 130, 143, 145
information, 36, 57, 67, 84, 94, 107, 149, 151, 157, 158
ingenuity, 91
initiative, 27, 47, 52
injury, 78, 79
innovation, 3–5, 7, 12, 14, 15, 17, 20–23, 25, 27, 30, 35, 38, 42, 43, 45, 47, 49, 50, 52, 53, 55, 62, 65, 67, 76, 78, 104, 117, 119, 125, 127, 129–132, 134, 142–145, 152, 154, 156, 159
innovator, 3, 5, 12, 25, 46, 53, 127, 130, 132, 134
inquiry, 15, 143
inspiration, 6, 119, 121, 144

instance, 1, 21, 26, 28, 29, 52, 55, 66, 78, 84, 85, 87, 88, 91, 114, 115, 123, 127, 130, 136, 144, 145
integration, 21, 25, 30, 37, 56, 61, 62, 65, 67, 68, 70, 71, 73, 77, 78, 80, 85, 86, 88–92, 94, 100, 107, 113, 114, 149, 156, 157
integrity, 80
intelligence, 53, 70, 88, 91, 144, 156
interaction, 32, 35, 43, 62, 66, 74, 75, 79, 91, 147, 156, 158
interactivity, 29, 35, 38, 57, 62, 152
interconnectedness, 73
interest, 1, 2, 14, 15, 24, 51, 52
interface, 27, 55, 57, 133, 144
interference, 27, 68, 84, 92, 107, 157
intern, 126
internet, 16
interplay, 3, 15, 134
intersection, 20, 27, 51, 86, 130, 142, 149, 152
intervention, 69
investment, 37
isolation, 87, 99, 101, 103, 140, 151
issue, 26, 66, 124, 140
iteration, 152

Java, 16
job, 151
John Rawls, 104
journey, 3–5, 12, 14, 15, 17, 22, 24, 25, 27, 30, 44, 46, 50, 53, 55, 83, 99, 115, 119, 120, 127, 130, 132, 134, 137, 143–146, 159
justice, 104–106, 115, 143

Kai, 1–5, 7, 12, 14–16, 23–27, 44–46, 53–55, 130–132, 134, 144–146
Kai Ba, 5, 6, 9, 12, 14, 20, 22, 25, 27, 30, 41, 43, 44, 47, 50, 51, 53, 55, 57, 60, 65, 67, 119, 121, 125, 127–130, 132–137, 139, 142, 145, 146
Kai Ba's, 1–5, 7, 17, 22, 27, 46, 49, 119–121, 123, 125, 128–135, 141–146
key, 1, 7, 41, 44, 46, 65, 71, 92, 144, 152
knowledge, 3, 15, 23, 42, 73, 123, 125, 127, 130, 144, 146

lab, 24, 41–46, 48–52, 125–127, 131
lack, 119, 150
landscape, 20, 27, 47, 78, 80, 85, 86, 88, 91, 96, 109, 111, 115, 121, 125, 130, 139, 141, 147, 154
language, 24
laser, 29
latency, 65, 66, 84
launch, 127, 133
Layla, 120
leader, 26, 50, 51
leadership, 49
league, 79
learning, 3, 16, 23, 25, 26, 28, 35–37, 46, 57, 60, 62, 70–73, 120, 124, 126, 145, 155, 156, 158
legacy, 119, 123, 125, 130–132, 141–143, 146, 157–159
leisure, 135

Index 169

length, 29
lesson, 17
level, 155
lie, 22
life, 2, 4, 12, 14, 25, 88, 94, 100, 102, 104, 105, 107, 109, 114, 134, 135, 137, 142, 143, 151, 156, 158
lifestyle, 137
light, 7, 27, 50, 65, 68, 92, 107, 141, 144, 157
Lila Chen, 26, 27
limit, 29, 68
limitation, 150
living, 143
location, 69
love, 3, 145

machine, 70, 88–91
making, 37, 43, 89, 124, 126, 129, 130, 151
management, 37, 86
manner, 28, 92
manufacturing, 36
mapping, 33
march, 14
mark, 119, 125
market, 36
marketability, 23
Mars, 36, 84–88
Marshall McLuhan, 143
mastery, 158
materiality, 77
means, 20, 113, 114, 143, 159
measure, 144
mechanism, 140
medicine, 68
medium, 29, 30, 68, 143
member, 126

mentee, 26
mentor, 27, 120
mentorship, 3–5, 25–27, 119, 121, 125, 143, 145
merging, 115
message, 143
metric, 62
mind, 1
mindset, 17, 53, 55, 119, 121, 145
miscommunication, 23
misdiagnosis, 69
mission, 41–45, 52, 84–86, 119, 126
misuse, 80, 158
model, 28, 91, 116
module, 22, 57
monitoring, 117, 141
Moon, 85
mortality, 114
mother, 1
motion, 37
myriad, 6, 86, 150

narrative, 74
nature, 3, 5, 25, 29, 75, 78, 114, 115, 125
necessity, 144
need, 27, 37, 38, 66, 68, 83, 84, 105, 107, 115, 135, 142, 144, 150
network, 45, 125
networking, 131
neuroscience, 52
Nick Bostrom, 86
Noteworthy, 129
novel, 37
novelty, 37

object, 92, 107
obligation, 96, 145

observation, 15, 39
obstacle, 134
olfactory, 159
oncology, 69
operating, 156
opportunity, 14, 26, 111, 144
option, 133
orbit, 91
orientation, 56, 77
other, 30, 44, 56, 125, 157
outcome, 22, 73
output, 136, 155
outreach, 52
overload, 73

pace, 57, 117, 144
packaging, 29
pandemic, 124
panel, 125
paradigm, 73, 74, 111, 152
paradigms, 144, 147
part, 55, 60, 130
participation, 42, 77
partnership, 21, 52, 127
passion, 1, 4, 12, 14–17, 26
past, 156
path, 3, 16, 22, 26, 27, 55, 132, 134
patient, 19, 62, 68–70, 126
pattern, 26, 68, 107
perception, 29, 63, 157
performance, 37, 62, 67, 78–80, 127, 150
perseverance, 4, 53
perspective, 65
Peter Singer, 145
phase, 44, 47, 141
phenomenon, 107
philosopher, 86, 143
philosophy, 27, 139, 142

physics, 1, 15, 19, 155
pillar, 25
pilot, 25
pioneer, 3, 26, 132, 139
plan, 28
planet, 83, 86, 88, 113
planning, 66, 86
platform, 14, 19, 20, 22, 41, 57, 59, 60, 62, 65, 67, 85, 88, 105, 114, 125, 126, 131, 133, 140, 144, 145, 149
play, 78, 80, 85, 104, 125, 157
player, 78
plethora, 125
policy, 115–117
pooling, 52
potential, 2–5, 9, 17, 20, 26–33, 35–37, 45, 51, 59–62, 68–70, 72, 73, 75, 78, 79, 82–84, 87, 88, 90, 91, 93, 94, 97, 99, 100, 102–107, 109, 110, 114–116, 124, 130, 134, 149–151, 153–156, 158, 159
power, 22, 27, 41, 67, 109, 139, 142, 144–146, 152
practicality, 29
practice, 22, 68, 70, 78, 85, 88, 126, 156, 158
precedent, 25, 134
precipice, 115
precision, 28, 150
preparedness, 85
presence, 36, 43, 63, 74, 84, 85, 157
present, 26, 36, 76, 84, 115
pressure, 84, 87, 133
principle, 27, 44, 92, 105, 116
privacy, 23, 29, 40, 62, 67, 79, 86, 94, 96, 106, 109, 134, 149,

Index

150, 158
privilege, 105
problem, 24, 26, 55, 60, 85
process, 24, 35, 36, 44, 45, 55, 57, 65, 68, 145
processing, 62, 66, 150
product, 29, 36, 119, 127
production, 36, 149
productivity, 46, 109–111
professional, 27, 55, 136, 137, 146
program, 2, 16, 85, 124
programming, 16
progress, 30, 119, 121, 127, 134, 144
project, 14, 18, 20, 23, 27, 28, 45, 46, 65, 76, 88, 120, 124
promise, 28, 33, 154
propagation, 65, 133
property, 36
proportion, 76
protection, 39
prototyping, 36
prowess, 51
psychologist, 53, 145
psychology, 20, 23, 60, 86, 142
public, 24, 83, 94, 115–117, 124, 133, 134, 141, 143
purpose, 45, 137
pursuit, 15, 63, 134, 135, 144, 146
push, 7, 41, 47, 64, 68, 130

quality, 21, 29, 36, 37, 63, 142, 150
quantity, 21
quest, 62
question, 115, 123

race, 119
range, 60, 79, 131
rapid, 27, 31, 117, 133, 144
rapport, 84

rasterization, 65
Ravi Patel, 126
Rawls, 105
ray, 65
re, 79
realism, 62–65
reality, 4, 17, 23, 26, 40–42, 44, 57, 65, 83, 86, 88, 97, 109, 115, 123, 124, 126, 130, 131, 156, 158
realm, 3, 14, 25, 29, 50, 62, 65, 78, 94, 104, 114, 132, 139, 143, 145, 149, 154, 156
reasoning, 60
recognition, 50, 56, 128, 148
reconstruction, 27, 68
recording, 27, 29, 68
recovery, 79
recruitment, 45
reduction, 159
reevaluation, 115
refinement, 67
reflection, 35, 36, 73, 144, 157, 159
refresh, 150
regulation, 115–117
rehabilitation, 52, 78, 80, 126
relation, 39
relationship, 39, 43, 143, 151
relay, 119
relevance, 62, 124, 128
reliability, 69
reliance, 77, 91
relief, 102
reminder, 125, 134, 137
rendering, 50, 65–67, 133, 150
report, 140
representation, 14, 18, 50, 77, 79, 92, 104, 106, 107

research, 4, 17, 20, 23, 26, 47, 48, 52, 68, 70, 83, 85, 88, 91, 128
researcher, 4
resilience, 16, 17, 22, 27, 53, 55, 144, 145
resistance, 37, 125
resolution, 29, 46, 150
resolve, 133
resonance, 57
resource, 24, 46, 49, 66, 77, 86, 111, 113, 149
respect, 46
response, 24, 25, 38
responsibility, 27, 43, 51, 52, 115, 130, 139, 141, 142, 144–146
result, 119
retail, 37
retention, 25, 36
retreat, 45
return, 85
richness, 84
right, 45
rise, 79, 115, 150, 158
risk, 22, 77, 79, 85, 105, 114, 126, 151, 156, 158
Robert Friedland, 27
role, 1, 15, 21, 25, 48, 50, 55, 70, 78, 80, 86, 125, 130

s, 1–5, 7, 12, 15–17, 22–27, 29, 42–46, 48–53, 67, 69, 78, 86, 88, 119–121, 123, 125, 126, 128–135, 141–146, 150
safety, 66
satisfaction, 136
scale, 67, 76, 156
scenario, 86, 115
scene, 65
school, 1, 2, 15, 52, 123, 125
science, 1–3, 5–7, 23, 44, 126, 130
scratch, 16
section, 1, 3, 5, 20, 25, 27, 44, 53, 62, 65, 76, 91, 94, 99, 104, 109, 111, 115, 119, 123, 127, 132, 141, 147, 150
security, 23, 28, 29, 67, 86, 94, 96, 134, 149, 151, 158
selection, 45
self, 16, 114
Sen, 105
sensation, 57
sense, 2, 3, 16, 27, 43, 82, 84, 115, 158
sensitivity, 29, 84
sentiment, 15
series, 14, 24, 50, 123, 127
set, 3, 17, 25, 134
setback, 17
setting, 26, 79, 85
settlement, 88
share, 24, 146, 156, 158
sharing, 67, 69, 131, 143
shift, 70, 73, 74, 76, 107, 110, 111, 152, 154
shooting, 78
shopping, 37
show, 43
sickness, 37
significance, 12, 20, 127
simulation, 42, 86, 87, 115
size, 69
skepticism, 23
skill, 155
sleep, 135
soccer, 79

Index 173

society, 20, 32, 45, 51, 99, 102, 104–106, 109, 127–129, 141, 143, 152, 157, 159
socio, 86
sociology, 86, 142
software, 22, 30, 37, 65, 67, 84, 124, 150
solution, 150
solving, 24, 26, 55, 60, 65, 85
sound, 57, 63
source, 5, 16, 120
space, 36, 56, 76, 82–86, 88–91, 94
speaking, 124, 143
speech, 51
spirit, 27, 121, 130–132
stage, 3, 17, 44
stance, 141
stand, 30, 115, 141
state, 63, 155
statement, 51
status, 115
step, 44, 46, 85
Steve Jobs, 27
stone, 17
storage, 67, 151
storming, 44
story, 130
storytelling, 7, 74, 76
strategy, 24, 45
stress, 103, 133
stroke, 52
struggle, 66, 124, 150
student, 19, 127
study, 16
subsection, 12, 17, 23, 57, 68, 83, 89, 97, 107, 126
success, 17, 22, 24, 27, 44, 47, 50, 52, 53, 88, 119, 120, 124, 125, 127, 135, 137, 145

sum, 22
summary, 5, 134
summer, 16
sunlight, 77
superposition, 107
support, 4, 17, 73, 115, 119, 124, 146
surface, 36, 65
surrounding, 29, 104, 149
sustainability, 78, 111, 113, 131, 149, 159
synergy, 20, 62
synthesis, 5
system, 24, 28, 67, 86

tailor, 37, 69
tale, 7
talent, 45
tapestry, 12, 146, 156, 159
teacher, 1, 2, 73
teaching, 125
team, 12, 21, 23, 24, 44–46, 53, 56, 57, 65, 68, 84, 144, 146
teamwork, 2, 83, 85, 86, 124
tear, 78
tech, 52, 124, 125, 127
technique, 27, 68
technology, 1–5, 9, 12, 14–17, 20–27, 29–32, 35–38, 40, 41, 43–48, 50–52, 55, 60, 62, 63, 68, 70, 73, 75–80, 83, 85, 86, 88, 91–94, 96, 99–102, 104, 107, 109, 113–117, 120, 121, 123–128, 130–134, 139–146, 148–152, 154, 156, 157, 159
telescope, 1
tendency, 102

testament, 27, 55, 127, 130, 144, 157
testing, 66, 67, 133
text, 42
theory, 42–44, 86, 104
thinking, 4, 15, 24, 26, 67, 123, 146
Thompson, 2
thought, 41, 51
threat, 144
time, 28, 43, 61, 62, 65, 66, 69, 78, 83–85, 132, 135, 150, 151
tomorrow, 121
tool, 7, 9, 29, 37, 120, 123
torch, 132
Torres, 4
tourism, 37
town, 1
tracing, 65
tracking, 33
traction, 145
trainee, 62
training, 19, 22, 25, 27, 37, 62, 68, 70, 73, 78–80, 84, 85, 124, 126, 156, 158
trajectory, 25, 115
transfer, 39, 127
transformation, 74, 86, 97, 115
translation, 84
transparency, 39, 139–142
transport, 29, 65
trauma, 115
treatment, 68–70, 131
trend, 149
trust, 66, 84, 86, 96
Tupac Shakur, 156

underpinning, 57
understanding, 2, 15, 17, 19, 24, 26, 35, 41, 44, 57, 65, 66, 68, 69, 76, 83, 84, 96, 99, 104, 113–115, 134, 142, 144, 146, 154, 156, 157
universe, 1, 83, 91, 156
university, 52, 124
upgrade, 74
usage, 67, 77, 113, 141, 151, 158
use, 28, 29, 32, 36, 40, 57, 66, 68, 77, 78, 85, 86, 99, 115, 134, 145, 149, 156, 158
user, 21, 29, 37–40, 57, 60–62, 65–67, 109, 133, 140, 144, 147, 149, 150, 156, 158
utilization, 150

validation, 69
value, 4
venture, 152
versatility, 31, 33, 72
viewer, 65
viewing, 29
virtuality, 158
virtualization, 111, 113, 159
visibility, 55
vision, 3, 5, 7, 22, 23, 26, 41–44, 68, 88, 131, 132, 144, 146
visual, 21, 50, 57, 62, 66, 84, 152
visualization, 76, 78, 94, 157
voice, 24, 56

waste, 113
wave, 27, 121
wavefront, 68, 133
way, 17, 18, 28, 37, 46, 60, 70, 79, 83, 84, 86, 88, 91, 94, 109, 126, 147, 150, 154, 156
wear, 78
weight, 133

well, 30, 40, 63, 80, 87, 104, 117, 134, 135, 137
whole, 86
willingness, 22
wind, 77
wing, 4
wisdom, 26
woman, 120
wonder, 3
work, 12, 17, 24, 25, 40, 53, 60, 109, 111, 119, 123–125, 128, 129, 134, 135, 141, 143, 145, 146, 151
workflow, 36
workforce, 125, 151
working, 85
workshop, 123
world, 1, 2, 15–17, 33, 35, 40, 41, 44, 50, 60, 63, 65, 78, 79, 86, 89, 90, 97, 99, 102, 104, 113–115, 119, 124, 125, 127, 134, 143, 144, 146, 151, 154, 159
worldview, 12